meet the queen of sheba

meet the queen of sheba

of sheba

more dramatic portraits of biblical women

ROSANNE GARTNER

Judson Press

Valley Forge

meet the queen of sheba:
more dramatic portraits of biblical women

Bible quotations in this volume are from the following versions:
The New King James Version. Copyright © 1972, 1984 by Thomas Nelson Inc.
The *Holy Bible,* New Living Translation, copyright © 1996. Used by permission of
    Tyndale House Publishers, Inc., Wheaton, IL 60189. All rights reserved.
The Contemporary English Version. Copyright © 1991, 1992, 1995 by American
    Bible Society. Used by permission.
The Living Bible, copyright © 1971. Used by permission of Tyndale House Publish-
    ers, Inc., Wheaton, IL 60189. All rights reserved.

Library of Congress Cataloging-in-Publication Data
Gartner, Rosanne.
    Meet the Queen of Sheba : more dramatic portraits of Biblical women /
Rosanne Gartner.
        p.   cm.
    Includes bibliographical references (p.).
    ISBN 0-8170-1395-4 (pbk. : alk. paper)
    1. Women in the Bible—Drama.   2. Bible—History of Biblical events—
Drama.   3. Religious drama, American. I. Title.
PS3557.A7959 M44   2001
812'.6—dc21   2001029290

Printed in the U.S.A.

07 06 05 04 03 02 01

10 9 8 7 6 5 4 3 2 1

Contents

Preface

Not too many years ago my oldest son, Bill, gave me a book for Christmas. He knew of my interest in the women who walk the pages of Scripture, so his gift was about them. I have always cherished what he wrote in the flyleaf:

> Mom—
> I believe you'd be in the Bible—a "Woman of the Bible"—
> but you're just too young!
> Love always,
> Bill

To the casual observer, women played a minor role in God's plan, but a closer look can be revealing, even startling. The women who walk the pages of *Meet the Queen of Sheba* cover the entire social structure. There are skeptics and queens, mothers and business women. There is even a prostitute. As I have researched the lives of these women, the Lord held up a mirror to me. No, I am not a prostitute, but I am a sinner saved by grace. I am not a queen, but I am a child of the living God. I challenge you to see something of yourself as you read the real-life adventures of these women. I guarantee you will be surprised and, I pray, blessed.

Acknowledgments

My husband, Bud, and I live in a little house on a quiet street in a suburb of Chicago, Illinois. Well, it used to be quiet, but our neighborhood is changing. No, the "gangs" are not moving in. Our modest neighborhood is changing into an upscale North Shore community, so that our little house seems to be sinking into obscurity. I'll always remember the morning I realized I could no longer see the sunrise from my bedroom window. Our new neighbor's oversized house blocked the view. I cried.

The first thought occurs to you—take the money and run. In other words, when the next developer approaches you with an attractive offer, sell and move. Many of our neighbors have already done that. But after prayer and reflection, Bud and I agreed we'd stay. This is not merely a house; this is our home!

Oh, we have made an addition. We hung four birdhouses in the southern awnings. Now we can watch God's little creatures, right through the windows of our little country cottage. It has given perspective to the changes that have taken place.

We know that change is inevitable, but even more important, we know the constancy of our Lord. I just want to acknowledge God's guidance in this work called *Meet the Queen of Sheba,* and to thank him for the perspective he gives in an ever-changing world.

Hints for Presenters

Very few things capture my imagination more than having the privilege of presenting women of the Bible. The settings vary, almost as much as the women I present. I enjoy the challenge, but do not want the disadvantage of not knowing the setting beforehand. Most of the presentations are made in churches, but there are exceptions. When you are preparing to present one of these women, make certain of the following things:

1. *Know the material.* Become so familiar with the material that you can "get inside her skin." Merely reading the story from the book loses its appeal. In fact, don't use the book. Instead, make copies of the pages you need.

2. *Decide whether or not to have a podium.* Don't hold the pages, but put them on a podium (even a music stand will do). The less visible the script is to the audience, the more effective your presentation will be.

3. *Use a microphone.* I find the cordless, lapel microphone the best because I am not confined to one position, especially since I frequently move about as I perform.

4. *Minimize costumes and props.* I have always kept costumes and props simple: a crown for a queen, a simple dark dress for a peasant, a scarf, a water jug. I make exceptions on occasion. The

Queen of Sheba is more commanding if she is regally attired and has the appropriate makeup (yes, makeup was part of her culture). But I have always been more comfortable when I have kept costumes and props simple, my desire being to focus on the woman and her story.

5. *Draw your audience into the story.* Make eye contact with them, ad-libbing on occasion if necessary.

6. *Create a cast.* Consider having a partner off-stage who can be the voice of a character other than the woman you are portraying. This is particularly effective if the other character is a man.

7. *Add special touches.* Here is where your individuality can shine. Do you sing? Try ending a profile with a simple chorus that ties in with the story or that extends an invitation to accept or deepen one's relationship with Christ. This has been a very effective conclusion on many occasions.

8. *Be prepared.* People always want to know more! Be prepared to answer questions, but don't be afraid to say, "That's a good question. Let me look in to it." Then be sure to follow up by finding the answer, if indeed there is one. Remember, God doesn't tell us everything!

9. *Modify the script.* The hardest thing for me to do is to cut something from a script, but sometimes the story is longer than the audience has time for or desires. At the beginning of each story, I have indicated the approximate time it will take to present the material orally. If the storytelling would take longer than thirty minutes, the following suggestions might prove helpful. You'll find suggestions as well for off-stage voices that can enhance your reading.

Suggestions for individual stories:

DEBORAH

She can tell her story in approximately thirty minutes. Besides Deborah, there are two male characters: her husband and Barak. If you would like to have an off-stage voice, Barak would be very effective.

HANNAH

This prayer warrior tells her story in approximately thirty minutes. Besides Hannah, there are two characters who speak: her husband

and her adversary. Either one or both would be very good off-stage voices if you so choose.

THE WITCH OF ENDOR

She tells her story in approximately thirty minutes. If you choose to have an off-stage voice, Samuel would be very effective.

THE QUEEN OF SHEBA

The Queen of Sheba's story takes about thirty minutes. The voice of Solomon off-stage could be very effective.

GOMER

Gomer tells her story in about thirty minutes. Hosea's voice off-stage could be very effective, particularly if you just use the voice for prophecy.

ESTHER

If you present her whole story, it will take approximately forty-five minutes. I have found her story more effective when I have included a tradition from the Feast of Purim, which adds another five minutes.

Before you begin your presentation, distribute noisemakers and explain briefly to your audience that, in the Jewish faith, the Feast of Purim remembers the account of how Esther and Mordecai foiled Haman's plot to destroy the Jews on a day decided by the drawing of lots (in Hebrew, this was called *purim*). Explain that to this day, when the Book of Esther is read at Jewish worship services, the congregation tries to drown out the sound of Haman's name by hissing, stomping their feet, and rattling noisemakers.

In this monologue, Haman's name is first mentioned when Mordecai tells Esther about revealing a plot to murder the king (at the end of the paragraph beginning with the words "I was appalled . . ."). At the first mention of the name Haman, rattle your noisemaker and signal the audience to do the same. With the words, "Ultimately, the battle was the Lord's . . ." I put my noisemaker down to signal the conclusion of that part of the story.

Here are some cuts you can make to shorten the story:

1. Eliminate the palace description and the poem at the beginning of the story. Begin with the paragraph that starts, "King Xerxes' reputation for his ostentatious celebrations . . ."

2. Omit the section beginning, "Was the crown the only adornment . . ." Resume the story with the words, "What did she do, Father?"

3. Omit the paragraph beginning, "But I was comforted . . ." Resume the story with the paragraph beginning, "Finally the day for that appearance arrived."

4. Omit the poem at the end of the story.

CLAUDIA PROCULA

To do the entire story of Pontius Pilate's wife, you'll need an hour. The voice of Pontius Pilate would be most effective. Several cuts can be made, however, that would reduce the time to approximately forty minutes.

1. Read the first and third paragraphs to open the story, eliminating the following two paragraphs, and pick up the story again where the paragraph begins, "As I have said, I am proud of my name. But sadly, I am not so proud of my husband's."

2. Continue for several pages, until you come to the paragraph that starts, "'Its history,' he said, 'and its strategic location cannot be equaled!'" Eliminate everything that follows until the paragraph that begins, "Nothing was left to chance when Antonia was built." Take up the story there.

3. Continue for several more paragraphs. Cut the section that begins, "Moments later Julia told me about the legend of Jericho." Resume the story where it says: "At last Pontius turned to his aide who stood attentively at the governor's side."

4. The next cut begins at the paragraph starting with, "In the meantime, I was keen to learn all that I could about the Jews." After cutting the next several paragraphs, resume your reading with, "While I was keen to learn about the Jews, Pontius was certain he had them all figured out."

5. Next cut is the paragraph that begins, "Dorcus told me of a strange group of people—the Essenes." Your reading resumes with the words, "'I have heard about Jesus,' I said. 'Tell me about him. . . .'"

6. There is not another cut until you come to the paragraph that starts, "Jesus came to Jerusalem. He celebrated the Passover with

his disciples." Resume your reading with the words, "I did not know at the time that Jesus had to die."

If you have only about thirty minutes, read the first, third and sixth paragraphs to open the story, and then pick up the monologue with the paragraph that begins, "We had barely settled into the palace in Caesarea, when Pontius made plans to visit Jerusalem. . . ." Continue the story, making the cuts indicated above.

SALOME, MARY MAGDALENE, JOANNA

This story takes approximately forty-five minutes to present orally. It is best done using three women. It works well in three fifteen-minute sessions. Each session has one monologue by each of the women. The first session tells how each woman met Jesus; the second tells an experience each had with the Master. The third and final session speaks of the three women going to Jesus' tomb on Easter morning.

EUNICE

Eunice tells her story in approximately forty minutes. Paul, Barnabas, Lois and Timothy are the other characters in the story. Any one or two off-stage voices would be very effective. There are cuts that can easily be made that would reduce the reading to approximately thirty minutes.

1. Begin the first cut at the paragraph that starts, "That was a real blessing because we didn't have a synagogue . . ." Resume the reading with the paragraph that begins with the words, "It was interesting that my husband, who did not object . . ."

2. After reading that paragraph, your next cut begins with the following paragraph that starts, "Our village was on a small hill about one hundred feet above the fertile valley . . ." Pick up the story again with the paragraph that begins, "Timothy was hardly in his teens when his father died."

3. Read on until the paragraph that begins, "As we made our way down the path, Lois recited . . ." Five paragraphs later, resume your reading with the words, "Paul was the younger of the two men . . ."

4. Cut the section that begins with, "'Did you hear what Paul said?' Timothy asked, his face aglow . . ." Begin again with the words,

"Barnabas, who stood tall and dignified, smiled warmly at Mother Lois."

5. The final cut begins with the paragraph that reads, "We heard reports of their work in Perga and Attalia." Resumption is with the paragraph that begins, "But the Lord kept us in Lystra where we continued to work . . ."

LYDIA

Lydia tells her story in just over thirty minutes. As in the story of Eunice, Paul is a strong character for an off-stage voice.

CHAPTER 1

Deborah

Mother of Israel

"Everyone has a calling," my husband, Lapidoth, would say. "And you, Deborah," he'd continue, shaking his head in mock disbelief. "You have been called to be a prophet of God."

Then, without another word, he'd put the blanket on my little donkey in preparation for my brief journey to the palm tree that lies between Bethel to the north and Ramah to the south.

"Ah yes, a prophet," I said, mounting my patient little animal. "But we live in a time of such turmoil and strife. Ehud was such an able judge, but he has been dead all these years."

"But," Lapidoth countered, "Israel knew rest for eighty years. And remember Shamgar? What a great blessing that he killed those six hundred dreaded Philistines!"

"With an ox goad, no less," I reminded him. "But look how the people again do evil in the sight of the Lord! They play the harlot with false gods—the Baals and the Ashtoreths. They are so quick to turn from the way in which their fathers walked. They no longer obey God's commandments."[1]

"I know," my husband agreed, "They just will not cease from doing it their own way instead of God's."

This story takes approximately thirty minutes to present orally.
For more ideas, see "Hints for Presenters" at the beginning of the book.

"They do what is right—in their own eyes," I added, leaving Lapidoth standing in the garden beside our modest mud brick home. It was only by God's good grace and guidance that I could judge the problems of these people.

Even without my prompting, my little donkey knew the way that we went each day. We rode the well-worn path easily from Bethel,[2] our home village. Like most of our villages, Bethel sits at the point of a low rocky ridge. Before long we arrived at my "court," beneath the stately palm tree; "Deborah's Palm Tree," people called it. It was the ideal location, between Bethel and Ramah. People came daily, bringing their concerns, their questions, their disputes.

"Deborah," I was asked, "if I buy a Hebrew servant, how long shall he serve me?"

"He shall serve six years," I said, "and in the seventh, he shall go free and pay nothing."[3]

"Why should I not labor or do any work on the Sabbath?" I was asked by another anxious Israelite.

"In six days the Lord made the heavens and the earth, the sea, and all that is in them, and rested the seventh day. Therefore the Lord blessed the Sabbath day and hallowed it,"[4] I explained.

One often-asked question that grieved me was, "Why is it an abomination to the Lord to serve other gods?"

My answer was a stern reminder: "You are a holy people to the Lord your God; the Lord your God has chosen you to be a people for Himself, a special treasure above all the peoples on the face of the earth."[5]

"We are crying out to the Lord," was their constant complaint. "We have been sold into the hand of Jabin, king of Canaan. And Sisera, the commander of his army, has continually and harshly oppressed us."[6]

"Your obstinacy and ingratitude toward the Lord has brought you to this state of wretchedness," I reminded them judiciously. "Until you repent you will continue to live in torment and continue paying tribute to Jabin. Repentance is your only hope!"

Their mournful cry was piteous beyond words, reaching the very heavens. "The yoke is too heavy! The burden too great!" was their unrelenting lament.

Twenty years of pain finally brought the first movements toward repentance to this stiff-necked people. There were signs all over the land that they were making attempts to return to the Lord, even abandoning the false Canaanite gods who had so severely enslaved them. They had imagined they could serve those abominable idols without offending the only true God, Yahweh.[7] How absurd! How foolish!

"At last," I cried, watching their humble attempts to restore their relationship with the Lord. "At long last."

Their signs of repentance gave me renewed vigor, and awakened my hope. I knew what I must do. I must remain close to the Lord, and seek his wisdom. As I sought his counsel, my faithful Lord made it clear. In obedience to God, I sent for Barak.

"Go," I ordered my servant, "Go to Kedesh, in the highlands of Galilee, to the tribe of Naphtali. There you will find the Lord's general, Barak. Tell him that I have received a message from Yahweh, and that he, Barak, must come to Bethel at once! There can be no delay!"

Once the Lord delivers a decree we must be quick to obey. I felt added urgency because Jabin, the Canaanite king, had increased his evil deeds in our land, sacking our villages, plundering, destroying.

"Is it not enough for him," I cried, "that he has oppressed us for lo these twenty years?"

As I continued to pray, the strength of the Lord became as a shield within my very being. In all of Israel, there were no shields, no chariots of iron, no long-range bows. Our people had only bronze and copper daggers, swords, slings and short-range bows. But now—I possessed the strength of the Lord. *This is the only shield we need!* I marveled.

At last my servant returned with Barak.

"Ah, General Barak," I said, "I have a message for you from the Lord God of Israel!"

"And what is that, Deborah?" he asked.

"The time has come for us to take action. The Lord has commanded that you gather ten thousand men from the tribes of Naphtali and Zebulun. You must lead them to Mount Tabor."

I could see the color drain from his face, but I continued. "We can be certain of one thing—that cruel general, Sisera, will be leading King Jabin's army. That arrogant Canaanite will come out in force to fight you at the Kishon River. And mark my words, he and his fighting men will have their chariots. But the Lord will trick him. He has promised to help you defeat the enemy. Victory is assured!"

My assurance was not matched by Barak. "*You* are God's agent," he said, a slight quiver in his voice. "Don't ask me to go—no—not unless you go, too!"

"What!" I demanded. "You would defy the word of the Lord?"

My decision was made. "All right, Barak," I said. "I will go! But I'm warning you, the Lord is going to let a *woman* defeat Sisera."

I watched as the edict made its impact on the once proud and capable general. Then, I told him, "No one will honor *you* for winning the battle." The final insult had been delivered. He did not respond.

Preparations were swift and thorough. The journey took us through the great city of Shiloh, six miles from Bethel. From there, we continued northward to the hill country of Ephraim, through Shechum in the pass between Mount Ebal and Mount Gerizim. On we traveled beyond Mount Gilboa, and then along the Sea of Galilee and past King Jabin's city, Hazor. Finally we reached Kedesh. What a welcome sight that village was, sitting regally on the graceful hill.

The Canaanites were everywhere to be seen, but they had so little regard for us that they were either unaware of or unconcerned about the mission Barak and I were undertaking.

"We have no time to lose," I told the general as we dismounted our sturdy donkeys. "The Lord has commanded that we muster ten thousand men and march to meet the enemy!"

I could see the concern in Barak's eyes. "We will be meeting a formidable enemy," he said.

"Fear not, Barak," I said in reproof. "The battle is the Lord's! No matter that Sisera has nine hundred chariots of iron. He could have nine *thousand!* And *one hundred thousand* men! Who is mightier than the Lord God Almighty?"

I turned then and left Barak to follow God's orders. He sent two of his ablest soldiers to enlist the men of the tribe of Zebulun to the south, while he himself mustered the men from his tribe, Naphtali. I was not surprised at the swiftness of the muster, for I knew, *I knew—* the battle was the Lord's.

Ten thousand men stood before Barak and me—farmers, herdsmen, craftsmen, hardly a soldier in the lot.

The strength of the Lord once again reassured me. I turned to General Barak and said: "Rise up! Take heart! For this is the day in which the Lord has delivered Sisera into your hand! Praise God, for he has already gone out before you!"

The words of encouragement exhilarated Barak, giving him a spirit of command. He turned to the volunteers standing before us. "Men of Israel," he shouted, confidence sounding like a mighty trumpet blast, "we shall march southwest, to Mount Tabor. It is time to come out from under the yoke of the Canaanites!"

A great roar of approval rose from the crowd of eager men. They had caught the zeal of the momentous occasion and were eager to meet the enemy.

Barak led the march, his head held high in his position as general of the army of God. Scouts were sent scurrying ahead to get the exact location of Sisera and his troops. The only sounds were those of marching feet and braying animals. We didn't speak much during the march, each of us lost in our thoughts and prayers.

The words of the Lord came to me as a great comfort, "The Lord will establish you as a holy people to Himself, just as He has sworn to you, if you keep the commandments of the Lord your God and walk in His ways."[8]

I was roused from my reverie to see one of our scouts returning. "Sisera is on the march," he announced breathlessly. "He has left his base at Harosheth on the Plain of Acre. He and his army are advancing in full battle array along the open plain past Megiddo and Taanach."

"He thinks to frighten us by his great martial strength," Barak noted.

"He is mistaken," I assured him. "See the rain clouds ahead. Our men will not grow fainthearted, for the Kishon River shall be our ally!"

Barak alerted our troops to be at combat ready just as we felt the first drops of rain. They were harbingers from the Lord, heralding the sweet dew of success. Soft and moist, they caressed my cheeks. My heart sang in delight for I knew that the Kishon River would overflow its banks as the rain continued. I knew that by the time we arrived in the valley to do battle with the Canaanites, the river would have escaped its banks and muddied the battlefield.

"Hurry!" I ordered as the rain increased its velocity, no longer soft and moist, but harsh and soaking; no longer caressing my cheeks, but pelting my face in its eager onslaught. I was delirious with joy! "This is the Lord's doing!" I shouted to Barak above the storm's fury.

"There, in the valley of Jezreel, awaits the enemy," Barak shouted as we hastened to meet them.

We quickened our pace, oblivious of the rain and wind. Our enemy came into view as specks of dust on the southern horizon. Our men were impatient to meet the foe and our zealous efforts were realized as we faced the enemy at last.

The Canaanites were desperately trying to begin an attack, but the confusion caused by the sudden storm and the mud it produced made it all but impossible.

"See!" I announced. "The chariots are helplessly bogged down in a quagmire of heavy muck."

"Attack!" Barak ordered as we charged headlong into the watery scene in a wild assault. The men of Israel fought with triumphant fury. Only the Lord could have accomplished such a one-sided victory! Our foe was completely off-balance, and their forces were routed and wiped out.

All but one enemy was destroyed in the melee. Sisera escaped, with Barak in full pursuit. I watched them as they fled toward the encampment of Heber the Kenite. We owed much to the Kenites, the tribe of traveling tinkers. It was they who taught our people the art of metal craft. Why, Moses' father-in-law was a Kenite! I recalled.

But their loyalties moved from people to people and from tribe to tribe. Most recently they seem to have developed a relationship with the Canaanites. It must be true, I thought, for now Sisera was on his way to Heber's encampment, with the General of God's army at his heels.

Did Barak recall my words, "No one will honor you for winning the battle"? I was certain that he wanted to redeem himself for his insistence that I accompany him into combat. Perhaps he hoped that his recent gallant actions would persuade the Lord to rescind his edict: "The Lord is going to let a woman defeat Sisera. No one will honor you for winning the battle."

It is true that Barak proved himself in battle, leading the charge with courage and fervor. And now, here he was, in his earnest quest to destroy our Canaanite rival, King Jabin's ruthless general, Sisera.

It stopped raining. It was no longer needed. The enemy was routed. I made my way toward the Kenite encampment in my own pursuit. As I neared Heber's tent, I saw Barak making his way toward me, alone.

"Hail, Barak," I called.

"Hail, Deborah," he responded.

"Is all well?" I asked. "Where is our enemy?"

"He is dead," the general said.

"You have slain Sisera?" I asked.

Barak lowered his eyes. "No," he said at last. "Not I, but Jael has slain him."

"What? Heber's wife? What happened?"

"Sisera went into her tent," Barak explained. "He asked for a drink of water. But Jael told me that she gave him a cup of milk instead. She knew what she was doing. The milk soothed him, and soon he was fast asleep. By the time I got here, she had already killed him."

"See how the Lord uses every circumstance to bring about his will!" I noted. "Sisera thought the Kenites were his friends, but God used Jael, a Kenite woman, to deliver justice to this wicked man.

"How did she slay him, Barak? Did she thrust a spear into his evil heart? Did she cut his throat with a lance?"

"No," the general replied. "She did neither. Instead she—ah—she took a tent peg in one hand and a hammer in the other." He paused briefly, then said in measured tones, "She drove the peg into his temple. The instrument of death made its way into the ground beneath Sisera's head."

"Bless the Lord," was all I could say.

God's victory cried out for a celebration. We rallied our triumphant troops. To honor the occasion I wrote a song. One which Barak and I sang together to celebrate the victory.

Hear, O kings! Give ear, O princes!
I, even I, will sing to the Lord;
    I will sing praise to the Lord God of Israel . . .
In the days of Jael, the highways were deserted,
And the travelers walked along the byways.
Village life ceased in Israel, until I, Deborah arose,
    arose a mother in Israel.
The people chose new gods; then there was war in the gates;
Not a shield or spear was seen among forty thousand in Israel.
My heart is with the rulers of Israel
    who offered themselves willingly with the people.
Bless the Lord! . . .
From Ephraim were those whose roots were in Amalek.

After you, Benjamin with your peoples,
    from Machir rulers came down. . . .
Zebulun is a people who jeopardized their lives
    to the point of death,
Naphtali also, on the heights of the battlefield.
The kings came and fought, then the kings of Canaan
    fought in Taanach,
By the waters of Megiddo;
    the stars from their courses fought against Sisera.
The torrent of Kishon swept them away,
    that ancient torrent, the torrent of Kishon.
O my soul, march on in strength! . . .
Most blessed among women is Jael, the wife of Heber the Kenite;
He asked for water, she gave milk;
    she brought out cream in a lordly bowl.
She stretched her hand to the tent peg,
    her right hand to the workmen's hammer;
She pounded Sisera, she pierced his head,
    she split and struck through his temple. . . .
Thus let all your enemies perish, O Lord!
But let those who love him be like the sun
    when it comes out in full strength![9]

Cheers arose from the brave soldiers, no longer farmers, herdsmen, craftsmen. Tears of pride and joy filled my eyes as I gazed upon the vast field of victory.

Then a voice from the crowd shouted, "O Deborah, Mother of Israel! Our hero, there is none like you!" Soon the words became a chant, then a roar: "Deborah, Mother of Israel! Deborah, Mother of Israel! Our hero!" The voice which began the chant was that of God's General, Barak.[10]

"You indeed are the hero," he told me later as I prepared to return to Bethel.

"But don't forget Jael," I reminded him. "The Lord sometimes uses unlikely people to fulfill his purposes, even a Kenite woman."

I returned to my palm tree between Bethel and Ramah and a life of peace, remembering that to achieve God's shalom it is often necessary to go through the rivers of strife. But he ever leads his people to ultimate victory.

"How shall we ever thank you?" the people asked upon my return.

"Thank our Lord," I responded, "and live grateful lives worshiping him, and none other. Remember the blessing Melchizedek gave Abraham—for it is our blessing too, as his descendants—'Blessed be Abram of God Most High, Possessor of heaven and earth; And blessed be God Most High, who has delivered your enemies into your hand.'"[11]

Who is your King Jabin? Who is your Sisera? The only way to live a victorious life is to live a life of obedience and trust. Whatever your circumstances, whoever your enemy, if you walk in obedience, trusting in the might and faithfulness of the one true God, then your victory is assured.

NOTES

1. The stories of Ehud and Shamgar are found in Judges 3:12–31. (All Scriptures in this chapter are quoted from The New King James Version.)

2. Scripture doesn't tell us if Deborah lived in Bethel or Ramah. It could have been either one.

3. Exodus 21:2.

4. Exodus 20:11.

5. Deuteronomy 7:6.

6. The biblical story about Deborah is found in Judges 4 and 5.

7. The holy name of God occurs in the Old Testament as a tetragrammaton YHWH, and is usually pronounced Yahweh. In Exodus 3:14, God declares this name to Moses. In its most literal and simple form, the name means "I am," signifying that the God of Israel is one who exists and who can never cease to exist. As such, Yahweh is trustworthy, not fickle like the gods of other nations. Yahweh is the same yesterday, today, and forever.

8. Deuteronomy 28:9.

9. Judges 5, paraphrased.

10. The Bible doesn't tell us this, but based on what the Bible does tell us, it is a logical conclusion.

11. This Abrahamic blessing is found in Genesis 14:19.

Hannah

Prayer and Praise

In days gone by, we had no king in Israel, and everyone did what was right in his or her own eyes. Although we had no king, we did have judges whom the Lord raised up when we got into trouble, or when other nations like the Philistines invaded our land. But we had no king, and as I said, everyone did what was right in his or her own eyes. Things were not good in Israel, and things were not good in our household. My dear husband, Elkanah, loved me very much, even more than he loved his other wife, Peninnah. Oh, how she hated me for that. And how she taunted me because she had so many children, and woe is me, I had none.

"Hannah!"[1] she would say. "What a fool you are to think that Elkanah really loves you. How can he? You are barren!" She loved that word *barren* and said it often. She would refer to me as Barren Hannah, and then she would laugh. All her children laughed too, for they knew it was a terrible shame to be a barren woman.

If it were not for Elkanah I think I would have gone mad in such a desperate situation. He loved me, and I clung to that reality, just as I clung to the reality of a just and merciful God.

This story takes approximately thirty minutes to present orally.
For presentation ideas, see "Hints for Presenters" at the beginning of the book.

When I was not crying out to Elkanah, I was pleading with my Lord. "O Lord," I prayed, "grant me the desire of my heart—a son! I bow before you in humble submission and pray that you would hear my earnest supplication."

We lived in our little mud-bricked house on a hilly slope at Ramah.[2] Our city was much like most other cities in Israel, built on the top of a hill. "For safety's sake," Elkanah would say.

The most important city in all of Israel was Shiloh,[3] for that was where the tabernacle[4] was located. The people of Shiloh were proud to be in the city where all the children of Israel came to worship. In addition, it was widely believed to be the first city that our ancestors built themselves.

"Joshua said we needed a special place for the ark," Elkanah explained to Peninnah's children, "so he instructed the people to build a city in the center of the land so that it would be accessible to all the Israelites."

In autumn our whole family would travel by donkey from Ramah to Shiloh. What excitement would run throughout our household as we made preparations for the fifteen-mile trip. It would take almost two days, but the journey was always worth the effort. After all, we were going to Shiloh to celebrate the Feast of Booths.[5] Year after year we would make our pilgrimage.

It should have been a time of great celebration, but Peninnah always made certain that my joy was diminished. Even as I prayed to the Lord of hosts, her persistent derision caused tears of anguish to flow unceasingly.

"Why do you cry, dear Hannah?" Elkanah would say to comfort me. "Do I not love you more than ten sons?"

I knew he spoke truthfully, but the ache in my heart was more than I could bear. I knew, even without Peninnah's mockery, that I was barren. Only God could change that, so I prayed with constant fervor. These thoughts were my constant companions, even as we journeyed once again to Shiloh, the sacred site for the tabernacle of the Lord that housed the ark of the covenant.

"Here's a good spot," Elkanah announced as he dismounted from his donkey. We all followed his lead. Soon we were busy erecting our booths using branches from trees that grew in abundance in the region surrounding Shiloh. My heart lightened as I set to the task, for I remembered God's mercy when our people were led out of Egypt.

"The booths represent freedom in our flight from slavery," Elkanah told the children. (He told them this every year as we erected our booths.) "We continue to celebrate each year at the time of harvest. Praise be to the Lord!"

Soon we assembled for a festival meal. As always, Elkanah divided the portions. And, as always, he gave me the greatest share to demonstrate his love for me. "O Lord," I prayed silently. "Why can't my joy be complete? Why have you withheld children from me?"

"Eat heartily and well, dear Hannah," Elkanah said.

But I did not miss the glare in Peninnah's cold eyes. "Yes, dear barren Hannah," she sneered, "eat heartily and well."

Laughter rose from the depths of her being as she mocked me. Her children joined her in mirthless chorus. Only Elkanah missed the abhorrent reason for the unkind merrymaking.

I tried desperately to keep the tears from escaping the sanctuary of my eyes, but several broke lose. I blinked them back. I began to rise from my seat next to Elkanah, but he gently took my arm to restrain me.

"Hannah," he said, "why do you weep? It breaks my heart to see you in such misery. Is my love not enough for you, dear one?"

"Oh, Elkanah," I cried, "forgive me. Your love is most precious, and the only comfort for a childless woman." Then my tears flowed freely. I not only felt the constant love of Elkanah, but the growing hatred of Peninnah.

Elkanah rose, and took my hands in his in a gesture of enduring love and mercy. "Hannah," he said, "you are the love of my life, my turtledove, all that I desire. You pray for a son; I pray for your happiness."

"I know, Elkanah. And I am ever grateful. But, I ache to have a child. If I am granted this gift, I shall return him to the Lord, to be his own Nazarite[6] forever. I shall go now to the tabernacle. There I will make my request to the Lord. Pray, Elkanah, pray that he will hear and answer!"

I made my way to the tabernacle, leaving my true love in the company of my everlasting tormentor. The tears would not stop. At last I reached the doorposts of the tabernacle. Eli the priest was sitting there beside the entrance.

I lowered my eyes and began my anguished plea, "O God Almighty, Lord of hosts, if you will look down upon my sorrow, and answer my prayer, and give me a son, then I will give him back to you." I continued silently, my lips forming the words of my petition. "My son will be yours for his entire lifetime. And as a sign that he is dedicated to you, Lord, his hair will never be cut."

My prayer was suddenly interrupted by a shout. "Hey, you!" Eli demanded, pointing an accusing finger. "Must you come here, to the tabernacle, in such a drunken condition?"

"Why, he thinks I've been drinking!" I was appalled at the thought.

"Throw away your wine!" Eli demanded.

"Oh no, sir!" I said. "I am not drunk. But I am so very sad. I was pouring my heart out to the Lord. Please, sir, do not think me a wicked woman! For I have been praying in great anguish and sorrow."

A look of understanding appeared in Eli's eyes, and he said with great conviction, "In that case, be of good cheer, dear lady! Turn from your despair. May the God of Israel grant the request you have made of him."

"Oh thank you, sir!" I said, feeling the warmth of hope.

I retraced my steps to be at Elkanah's side once again, the gloom of despair lifted, for the faith of the Lord had come upon me. "He will answer my prayer," my joyful heart sang.

Peninnah was prepared for my return, for her taunts resumed even as I entered our camp. "How was your visit to the tabernacle, dear barren Hannah?" Those words signaled the children's cruel laughter.

"My visit was fine," I told her. "Even Eli, the priest, spoke with me." My new confidence was evident to my foe. It confused her. It upset her. It silenced her.

The time for celebrating the Feast of Booths was coming to an end, but a different celebration took its place. The celebration of anticipation grew within me as I pondered the words of Eli, "Be of good cheer! Turn from your despair and may the God of Israel grant the request you have made of him." I knew that it was a word from the Lord.

Early in the morning on the following day, Elkanah, Peninnah, her children, and I went to the tabernacle to worship one last time before our return to Ramah. I had never felt the peace of the Lord as I did that beautiful autumn morning. The sun made its appearance in a radiance I had never noticed before, creeping gently over the nearby hills, cascading in hues of pink and orchid, creating a brilliant array of color that dazzled the tops of the trees in breathtaking tones of green and red. My heart sang as we made our way silently to the tabernacle.

> Mighty is the Lord God, a strong shield and a sun;
> Protecting, blessing, warming—the one to whom I run.
> I believe your promises, for you will never waver.
> You are a God bestowing honor and gracious favor.
> Lord, you withhold nothing from those walking in your path;
> Blameless and obedient, receiving not your wrath.
> O gracious Lord Almighty, your blessings overflowing
> For those who put their trust in you,
> and in your grace are growing.[7]

We made our way back to our home in Ramah. Everything was the same, but everything had changed, for I no longer viewed my world in despair and torment. I saw everything through the eyes of faith and hope. Elkanah was pleased with my lighter spirit and often remarked about the phenomenal change in my outlook.

"Oh, Elkanah," I said. "The Lord has heard my prayer. We will have a child, a son!"

"Hannah, Hannah," he said, enfolding me in his strong arms. "How many times have I told you that it matters not? I love you more than Peninnah and all her sons!"

Elkanah had accepted my barrenness, but I had not. His faith lay in the fact that God is gracious, even in denial of prayers. My faith lay in the fact that the Lord of hosts would grant my heart's desire. And when this child is born, I vowed, I shall return him to the Lord to be a servant of God for all his life!

As the weeks went by, it became apparent that God had answered my prayer. When I rose each morning, the nausea caused rejoicing in my heart, for I knew the bitterness in my stomach was the precursor to the sweetness of the birth of my son! Elkanah rejoiced with me. He was more attentive than ever. His joy matched mine.

I was very cautious during my pregnancy, following all the customs of our day. I refused hot baths for they might cause a miscarriage. I would not eat green vegetables, salty food, or fat. I did not want those things to adversely affect my unborn baby. The evidence of my "condition" soon became apparent to Peninnah. Her taunting ceased. Even her children began to treat me with feigned respect. Unloving as it was, I was grateful for it.

Even as my body grew heavier, my step grew lighter as the joy of the Lord swept me along, day after day, week after week. "Thank you, Lord," was my constant prayer.

"Elkanah," I whispered after a sleepless night. "By the mercies of God, send for the midwife. Our son will soon be born."

He wasted no time fulfilling my request, and before long, he returned with Iscah, the midwife, who aided in the birth of my son, bringing relief in my trial, restoration in my suffering, and consolation in my distress.

And then, through the surrealism of pain, my baby boy was born.

"My son," Elkanah said as he gazed upon the infant. Iscah carefully bathed, then rubbed salt on the tiny lad. Tears of joy coursed down Elkanah's cheeks.

"His arms and legs will grow straight and strong," he said as he watched Iscah wrap the swaddling cloths about the babe.

At last my son was placed in my arms. "Samuel![8] The Lord's child," I said. God's answer fulfilled, my promise assured. "He shall remain with us," I reminded Elkanah, "until he is weaned."

"Yes," my husband agreed, "and then you will keep your promise and present Samuel to the Lord at the tabernacle in Shiloh."

"And there," I added, "he will serve the Lord for all his life."

I had never known such joy as I experienced during those early days of Samuel's life. All the pain of the past was forgotten as I cared for my son. Peninnah hardly spoke to me now, and I found my heart going out to her. She had a grief I never experienced, for she was not loved as I was by Elkanah. My attempts to please her were often met with rebuff or scorn.

"You think you have won, Hannah," she would say. "But the day will come when you must keep your promise, and give Samuel to the Lord! Then what will you do?"

"I will see him each year when we go to Shiloh," I said. "And I will bring him a new coat each time, a coat that I will fashion for him myself." I was accomplished with needle and thread and had an eye for color, so I knew that my endeavors would be worthwhile. So did Peninnah.

The days and weeks went by so quickly, and before I realized it, it was time for the family to go to Shiloh for its yearly sojourn to celebrate the Feast of Booths.

"I won't be going this year, Elkanah," I said. "I will wait until the baby is weaned. Then I will take him to the tabernacle and leave him there with the Lord to remain forever."

"Whatever you think best, Hannah," he said. "Stay here for now, and may the Lord help you keep your promise."[9]

It was a solemn moment for me. I watched as the rest of the family made its way from our home, bound for the familiar road that led to Shiloh.

I enjoyed the quiet time alone with Samuel. "I shall cherish the memory of this time with my son as long as I shall live," I mused. His nearness refreshed and delighted me.

"Oh, Samuel," I would coo as I held him fast in my arms. "How gracious the Lord has been to me. To extend this gift is more than I can grasp. And, my darling boy, the gift shall be returned with deepest gratitude, for the Lord has removed my shame and covered me with his mercy."

The day of the family's return to Ramah thrust me back to the reality of our day-to-day lives. We were caught up in the routine of our home. Preparing the family meals was always a pleasure for me. The aroma of the lentil soup aroused everyone's appetite and before long we would all be seated cross legged around the mat that served as our table.

Elkanah would say the blessing, "Blessed are you, Lord God, King of the world, who causes bread to come forth from the earth."

He would be the first to dip his barley bread into the savory soup, and then each of us in turn would follow. There was always an ample quantity of vegetables, beans and lentils being the most abundant. On rare occasions meat or fish would be included in our simple fare, but fruit was always part of every meal, serving as dessert.

The sands of time flow relentlessly. Year after year, the family made their annual visit to Shiloh for the Feast of Booths. I watched dear Samuel grow into a fine little boy. He was finally weaned, but I was reluctant to part with him.

"Hannah, Samuel is weaned and on solid food," Elkanah reminded me. "It is time for you to keep your promise to the Lord."

"This time is bittersweet for me, Elkanah," I said. "I have been preparing for this day since the moment I conceived, but it is more difficult than I imagined."

"I know," he consoled. "But we shall see our little Samuel each year when we return to Shiloh. Come now, let us prepare for the journey. We must leave soon if we want to reach the city in time for the Feast of Booths."

Elkanah left just as Peninnah came into view. I realized that she had heard the conversation. "Yes, Hannah," she said, "it is time for you to keep your promise." She laughed as she continued, "You shall see your little Samuel, but only briefly, each year when we return to Shiloh." Her laughter echoed against the hills in mock gaiety. "Come now, let us prepare for the journey," she added viciously.

I could not respond, but turned and walked away, her cruel laughter following me as I went.

Things were not as bleak as some might think, for I, only I, knew that I was once again with child. The Lord was gifting me with a child once again. No one could ever replace my firstborn, but what a comfort knowing that another baby will fill my arms. That realization was a great solace for me as we made our way to Shiloh.

Upon arrival, we set up our booths as we had done so many times before. And, as was his custom, Elkanah spoke to the children about God's grace and mercy as he led our people out of Egypt. "And Samuel," he added, masking his emotions as best he could, "this year there is an added reason to sacrifice to Yahweh."

"What is that, Abba?" the boy asked.

"You, my son," Elkanah said, choking back the tears. "You are special to God, and the sacrifice we make this day is in your name to honor the Lord."

We made our way silently to the tabernacle for the sacrifice. We would offer the young bull we had brought from Ramah, along with some fine flour and wine.

The solemn sacrifice was completed under the watchful eyes of Eli, the priest. All the while Samuel stood between Elkanah and me, observing the ritual with rapt attention. I bent down to Samuel's level, as did Elkanah. I had told Samuel that the day had come—the day when he would begin to serve the Lord.

But he is so young! I thought. How can he even understand?

"Samuel," Elkanah began, "this is an important day—the most important day of your young life."

"Yes," I added, "this is the day you shall begin to serve the Lord.

You will be living here now, Samuel, in the tabernacle." I hugged my boy with the passion that only a mother can know.

I rose from my crouched position, as did Elkanah. Eli rose from his customary seat by the gate of the entrance of the tabernacle. Clearly, he was moved by the scene.

"O my lord," I said, "do you remember me? I am Hannah, the woman who stood on this very spot praying to the Lord." I took Samuel's hand and continued. "For this very child I prayed, and praise God, my petition has been granted! Now I am keeping the promise I made. I am giving this child to the Lord, and he will belong to the Lord as long as he lives."

Tears choked my words as I prayed, "My heart rejoices in the Lord; my horn is exalted in the Lord. I smile at my enemies, because I rejoice in your salvation. No one is holy like the Lord, for there is none besides you, nor is there any rock like our God . . . Even the barren has borne a child, and she who has many children will have no more . . . The Lord makes one poor and another rich; he brings down one and lifts another up. He lifts the poor from the dust—yes, from a pile of ashes! He treats them like princes, placing them in seats of honor. For all the earth is the Lord's, and he has set the world in order. He will protect the godly ones, but the wicked will perish in darkness. No one will succeed by strength alone."[10]

I looked down at Samuel, who now belonged to the Lord. "My darling," I reminded him, "God will protect you. Rely on him, and you will succeed in his strength." I hugged Samuel. So did Elkanah, lifting him in his strong arms. The three of us clung to one another for a brief moment.

Finally Elkanah put the boy down and said, "Be brave, be strong, Samuel, you are the Lord's boy."

"Yes," I added. "And remember, dear, we will be back next year for the Feast of Booths, and I promise, I will have a beautiful new coat for you."

We watched as Eli took Samuel's hand and led him into his new home, the tabernacle of the Lord.

We turned, reluctant to leave. But as we began to make our way back to Ramah, I felt the life of the new baby stirring within me. "Thank you, Yahweh," I whispered. "Thank you for your mercy and faithfulness."[11]

Are you hurting today? frightened? sin-sick? weary? What is your prayer? Turn to our Lord who does not withhold good things from his children. Trust our Lord who desires to pour out blessings upon you! Exhibit not only Hannah's faith, but Elkanah's as well. And may our Lord richly bless you.

NOTES

1. You will find Hannah's story in 1 Samuel 1:1–2:11.

2. In Hebrew, the town of Ramah is Ramathaim-zophim.

3. Shiloh was the leading city of Israel in the time of Samuel. It was probably destroyed by the Philistines in Samuel's lifetime, because he later set up his ministry in Ramah.

4. The tabernacle was the Israelites' place of worship, a tent that housed the ark of the covenant. The tabernacle was divided into two rooms, with an intricate veil to separate them. The inner room was called the Holy of Holies. It was there that the ark was kept.

5. Feast of Booths was the harvest festival that celebrated the covenant between God and God's people. For one week the people lived in small huts they made out of branches. The people celebrated with feasting, music, and sacrifices.

6. A Nazarite was a person consecrated to the Lord, separated from certain worldly things, such as wine or intoxicating drink. He also never cut his hair, as a symbol of his life of holiness. Samuel and John the Baptist were the only "Nazarites for life" mentioned in the Bible.

7. Psalm 84:11,12, poetically paraphrased.

8. Samuel, in Hebrew, means "name of God."

9. Elkanah was referring to Numbers 30:10–11, regarding a woman's vow.

10. 1 Samuel 2:1–9, paraphrased.

11. Hannah was blessed by the Lord with five more children. Her firstborn, Samuel, went on to become Israel's last judge and the nation's king-maker, anointing first Saul and then David. After anointing David, Samuel returned to Ramah, where he continued as judge and prophet.

CHAPTER 3

The Witch of Endor
Cabal from the Cave

I feel charming, oh so charming,

It's alarming how charming I feel.

I'm no beauty, not a cutie,

But, believe me, my charm is for real.

Why?

I have wisdom, uncommon wisdom,

My choice was shrewdly made.

Yes, my unique wisdom

Is important to my bewitching trade.

No doubt, you would not think me charming. You need to know, however, that there are those who call me a charmer. I believe that makes me charming. Although your perception of charming may be different, I think you will still have to agree that as a charmer, I am charming.

Actually, I have been called by many names besides charmer: witch, medium, spiritist, sorcerer. Take your pick. Personally, I prefer witch. It has a certain ring to it: Witch. And since I make my home in a cave in Endor, you may call me the Witch of Endor.

This story takes approximately thirty minutes to present orally.
For presentation ideas, see "Hints for Presenters" at the beginning of the book.

One thing about Endor, there is always plenty going on in the region. Unfortunately, the goings on are not very pleasant with all those Philistines constantly causing a ruckus. King Saul had his hands full. Of that, you can be sure. My cave is only about four or five miles from where the enemy was encamped. I was keenly aware of the many battles between the Israelites and those pesky Philistines. I could often hear the sounds of conflict in the valley below my humble abode.

Actually, I had made my home quite cozy, for a cave, that is. There are sturdy rocks along the west wall. I struggled to get them in place, but it was well worth the effort, because as I sat there, I could lean against the wall if I wanted to. I made a bed of soft twigs. I put my cape on top of the pile when I wanted to sleep. I don't have many belongings, so I must get as much use as I can from everything I own. But I must admit that my cape has seen better days. Oh well. What I really need is more patrons. That would ease the pinch I have been experiencing.

But in spite of everything, I am proud of the choices I have made. Being a witch is not the easiest of lives, but it has endowed me with a certain wisdom. I am a wizard, very wise and skilled.

Saul was the Hebrew's king. The Lord God had told the children of Israel that he, the Lord, was their King and their allegiance belonged to him. Yet, the Israelites were struggling with so many enemies that they wanted a human king, one they could see and hear. They knew the violence of their warring neighbors. They thought a king of their own was the answer. So they badgered the old prophet, Samuel. They clamored for a king! Finally, the Lord told Samuel to anoint a king for them—King Saul.

He was thirty years old[1] and the most handsome man in Israel—head and shoulders taller than anyone else in the land.[2]

I was in Gilgal on the day they crowned King Saul. It was clear from Samuel's message that neither he nor the Lord approved the Israelites' decision to rely on a human king.

Still, the people were encouraged when Samuel said, "Do not be afraid. You have certainly done wrong, but make sure now that you worship the Lord with all your heart and that you don't turn back on him in any way. Do not go back to worshiping worthless idols that cannot help or rescue you—they really are useless. The Lord will not abandon his chosen people, for that would dishonor his great name.

He made you a special nation for himself."[3] But Samuel's parting words sent a chill of apprehension into the hearts of the people. "If you continue to sin, you and your king will be destroyed."[4]

Saul's reign began with great promise. What a warrior he was— bold and fearless, mighty and cunning! One by one he defeated Israel's enemies beginning with the Ammonites, those fierce warriors from the northeast. He dealt courageously with the Edomites, Moabites and Amalekites as well.

The Philistines, however, always posed a formidable threat. Part of the problem was the Philistines' possession of iron and their ability to smelt it. Consequently, they had chariots, as well as weapons of war. We Israelites, on the other hand, did not. Our hapless army went into battle with little more than farm tools. There are only two swords in the whole of Israel. One belongs to King Saul and the other to his son Jonathan.

What started out so well began to sour when Saul disobeyed God. He performed the task of sacrificing a burnt offering—a task that only Samuel could perform. The news of Saul's verbal exchange with Samuel spread like wildfire throughout all of Israel. That old prophet put the fear of the Lord into King Saul all right.

"Your disobedience will cost you the kingship!" he said. And to add to the condemnation he told King Saul that if he had been true to the Lord, his kingship would have been established forever. The death knell of his reign sent Saul's spirits spinning into a decline that plagued him for the rest of his life.

Later on, Jesse's youngest son, David, came to the army's rescue in a tight situation. I learned about it from one of the king's officers who came to me for some of my "charm."

"That boy David killed the giant, Goliath," he told me. "With his slingshot and a few stones, of all things! Yes, sir! A slingshot and a few stones!" The officer scratched his head in disbelief, then added, "I saw him walk boldly out to do battle with Goliath, while that fearsome giant roared with laughter!

"'You think me a dog?' he said. That courageous lad never backed down. No sir-ree! He yelled right back at that Philistine, 'You, Goliath, come to me with sword, spear and javelin, but I come to you in the name of the Lord God Almighty—the God of the armies of Israel. Today the Lord will conquer you, and the whole world will know that there is a God in Israel! It is the Lord's battle, not ours, and today the Lord will give you to us!'

"And he did it!" the officer concluded. "He killed that giant and cut off his head."[5]

That incident was another of King Saul's thorny issues. Why? Because with time David's popularity soared while Saul's went into serious decline. I guess it didn't help either that Saul's son Jonathan became David's best friend. I heard that those two were inseparable, closer than brothers, you might say.

You know, I truly liked King Saul, but that rogue did one thing that really angered me. He expelled all the witches and mediums from the kingdom. If you could read a palm, or call up a spirit from beyond, you were gone!

"Don't go!" I begged my friend Timna, even as she gathered her meager possessions.

"I am sorry," she said, "I must go. It is too dangerous to stay here! If we are discovered, we shall be slain. Life is not good, but it is better than death."

She didn't even give me a farewell kiss, but quickly departed, her sack flung over her bent back. All right, Timna, go. See if I care!

But, I did care. I was frightened. Almost every medium packed up his or her wizardry and left Israel. I stayed. Tell me now, where was I to go? And, more importantly, how would I get there? I have never walked very far if I could help it, and riding a donkey is not my style. Besides, I had convinced myself that I was safe staying in my cave, right here in Endor, practicing my craft discretely and adding to my wisdom and wizardry.

> I will call up the spirits, hear what they say,
> I will practice wizardry day after day.
> Nothing's beneath my craft's clever schemes;
> I'll even tell you the meaning of dreams.
> Nothing can stop me for I have the glow.
> Each little secret I need to know.
> Incantations, spirit delights,
> Wisdom will bring me to greater new heights.

Wisdom is far above rubies, silver, and even gold. My heart was often warmed and thrilled with the realization that wisdom was the tool that enabled me to realize more rubies, silver, and gold.

My decision not to obey this new law and to stay in Endor, led to the most bizarre encounter of my entire life—my conclave with King Saul. It was just a brief meeting. We had never met before that awful night. But I'll tell you this much—that encounter changed both our lives. Why would King Saul want to see me, you might wonder, since he himself had banished witches from Israel? Aha! I told you I was charming!

I had heard that Saul and his army were in deep, deep trouble. Those pesky, persistent Philistines were at it again, more serious than ever. You've heard of "the last straw?" Well, I became King Saul's last straw.

I was about to retire on my bed of twigs when, in the dark of that fateful night, three strangers appeared at my cave. They were looking for my wizardry. I peered at them in the shadows. "Who are they?" I wondered. Two of the men were of medium height, but one of them, the one in the middle, was the tallest man I had ever seen. Why, I thought, he is as tall as King Saul!

Since I did not recognize them, I was very cautious. After all, practicing my trade could cause my death. So, I was careful. Remember, I wasn't even supposed to be in Endor, let alone work my craft.

"What do you want?" I said, surprised by the sound of my own voice.

The tall man, the one in the middle, answered, "This is urgent."

"What could be so urgent that would bring you here?" I demanded.

"Please," he pleaded, "I need to speak to someone." Then he lowered his voice, as though he were afraid that someone might overhear. "Please, Madam, conduct a—a séance for me," he said, his voice barely audible.

I was terror-stricken! A scream escaped my lips at the utter horror of the consequences of such an act. "Are you trying to get me killed?" I croaked. "Don't you know what King Saul has done? He has exiled all the wizards from Israel. And those who stayed behind, he has executed!"

I took a breath and peered at the trio before me. I raised my shaking hand and pointed an accusing finger. "You must be spies!" I cried in horror.

"No, no!" the tall one cried out. "I promise you, in the name of Yahweh, no harm will come to you. Please, I need your help! Please, help me!"

I hesitated, looking deep into the troubled eyes of this man who stood cowering before me. Compassion is not one of my attributes, but something about the pathos of this man cringing before me stirred a seldom-felt emotion.

"All right then," I said softly. "Whom is it you want me to bring up?"

Slowly, in measured words, he said, "Use your power, your wisdom, Witch." He seemed to struggle within himself for a moment before he said, "Bring up—Samuel—for me."

Those words struck me like a thunderbolt! The scream that welled up within my breast broke forth and echoed against the walls of my cave. "Samuel?" I cried in terror. "You have deceived me! I know who you are! You are Saul!"

"Do not be afraid," he insisted, reaching out to touch my arm. "No harm will come to you. I promise you." Again he pleaded, "Please, please, I implore you, bring up Samuel. Our army is in such disarray. I implored Yahweh for answers, but the Lord would not speak to me. And with Samuel now dead, I am beside myself with grief and worry. I need you to call up Samuel for me!"

"How did your aides discover who and where I am?" I asked him.

"All they said," Saul answered, "was that they had found a medium in Endor. I immediately disguised myself. I had to see you. I was desperate, Madam. I would allow nothing to keep me from this appointment. I had to come. Now, please, time is wasting. Call up Samuel for me. Now!"

The desperation in Saul's voice moved me to action. "As you wish, my king," I agreed.

Never, never, in all my charmed life has any spirit responded so quickly as did the prophet Samuel on that frightful night. My eyes widened with alarm at the specter. It was dreadful.

Saul saw the terror on my face. "What is it?" he demanded. "What do you see?"

"An old, old man," I cried.

The witch was bewitched!

"Look," I said, pointing to the apparition. "He is wearing a cape, a mantle." Yet another scream pushed its way through my fear-dried lips. "He is coming up!" I screamed. "Right up, out of the earth!"

"It is—it is—Samuel," Saul said, barely above a whisper. He fell to his knees, bowing low before the spirit.

I trembled at the sound of the voice emanating from within the spirit before me. "Why have you disturbed me, Saul?" he said in slow, even tones. "Why have you brought me back?"

Saul convulsed with fear. Then, with wavering voice, he finally addressed the spirit. "Oh Samuel, I am in deep, deep trouble. The war with the Philistines is going horribly. Everything is in disarray. And to make matters worse, God has left me. He won't reply, not by prophets nor by dreams. God is silent." Sobs of grief shook the distraught king as he pleaded, "Samuel! Samuel! I need your help. Please! Please tell me, what shall I do?"

The monotone of the spirit cried out, "Saul, Saul, why do you ask me? Remember your sin. Remember that God told you that the kingdom would be taken from you and given to David!"

Saul fell to his knees, his face to the ground.

Alarm struck my heart further when Samuel said, "What's more, Saul, the Lord himself will hand you over to the Philistines, and not only you, but the Israel army as well!"

Samuel's final words to the cringing king still ring in my head, "Tomorrow, Saul, you and your sons will be here with me. The Lord will bring the entire army of Israel down in defeat!"

Saul fell to the ground with those words. There was no doubt that he was filled with terror, remorse and, perhaps, conviction and repentance. He lay there, motionless. I could not bear the sight of the king lying prostrate at my feet.

"Come," I pleaded. "You must eat."

His aides added their pleas to mine. Finally he agreed. I prepared a meal that the three of them ate in eerie silence, each lost in his own terrible thoughts and imaginations. Then, in the darkness before the first light of day, they left.

I never saw him again. The next day, Samuel's prophecy became reality. Saul and his sons died in battle.

I often pondered Samuel's words, "Saul, you and your sons will be here with me."[6] I wonder, too, about my own future as I ponder in greater depth Samuel's words. Could they have this deeper meaning?

You, your sons will be here—For eternity.
Saul, you, your sons will be here—Will be right here with me.

Samuel's message poses—An interesting bent.
Did it give Saul the opportunity—To confess and to repent?

For we know that Samuel's future—Would be a heavenly place.
Perhaps our Lord in mercy—Extended tender grace.

A fearful proposition—That God can change a heart.
Is there hope for Saul, or for a wizard?—Is that where God's
  wisdom starts?

I am ever mindful of God's judgment, but even more than that, I am grateful for God's grace. I have experienced divine mercy, that while I was yet a sinner, God the Father sent his Son to die for me. I was given the twin gifts of faith and grace. With thankful heart I accepted them. God extended those same gifts to Saul and to the witch. The question is, did they accept them? God extends those same gifts to you. The question is, have you accepted them? Praise God, it is not too late.

NOTES

1. 1 Samuel 13:1. (Unless otherwise indicated, all Scriptures in this chapter are from the New Living Translation.)

2. 1 Samuel 9:2.

3. 1 Samuel 12:20–22.

4. 1 Samuel 12:25.

5. 1 Samuel 17:40–51, paraphrased.

6. 1 Samuel 28, paraphrased.

CHAPTER 4

The Queen of Sheba
Wit and Wisdom

Sheba is a land with a rich history of glory
and honor—a land whose people are of large stature and larger
heart—a land where women are equal with men, treated with
respect and dignity—a land whose gods, Almakah, Talbad, Kawim,
and most prominently, Attar, protect us and bless us with great
wealth. Much of the richness of Sheba is dependent upon our ability to trade and travel. Our trade caravans travel great distances to
trade in the choicest spices, gold, and all kinds of precious stones.
Did you ever wonder where frankincense and myrrh come from?
Sheba has the great fortune to have these much-valued trees in
abundance within our land.

She also has the great fortune to have me, the Queen of Sheba, as
her ruler! Please do not think me boastful when I tell you that my
beauty and wisdom are highly respected. But then, why not? I rule a
vast domain. My subjects include wealthy merchants and tradesmen.
Our mountainous land is in a strategic position between the Near
East and the Far East. It gives us a great deal of power.

This story takes approximately thirty minutes to present orally.
For more ideas, see "Hints to Presenters" at the beginning of this book.

There is power in wisdom, too. I believe that wisdom often stems from curiosity. I have an insatiable curiosity, which was aroused when I heard tales about a unique king, Solomon, the king of Israel.

"Tell me about him," I prompted my chamberlain following the repeated mention of his name. "Tell me what you have heard about Solomon."

Rehmah bowed in deference to his queen before replying. "Your Majesty," he said, "King Solomon is said to be the wisest man on the face of the earth. No one has surpassed his wisdom. His knowledge and acumen give rise to assumptions that his unprecedented wisdom is the gift of his gods."

My interest was further heightened with that assessment. "How can that possibly be true?" I wondered. After all, I had never met anyone as wise as me, let alone wiser! I do not say that to boast, but merely to have you understand the depth of my wisdom and my desire for more.

"Rehmah," I questioned, "can you give me an example of Solomon's learning, his knowledge, his wisdom?"

Rehmah thought reflectively for a moment, then said, "It has been said that he speaks words of wisdom such as, 'Good advice and success belong to me (wisdom). Insight and strength are mine. Because of me, kings reign, and rulers make just laws. Rulers lead with my help, and nobles make righteous judgments.'"[1]

I pondered Rehmah's words, the words of Solomon.

"Will you send your emissaries, Majesty?" Rehmah asked.

"No," I said. "I must meet this man. I must see and hear for myself such profound wisdom." I rose from my throne, resolute in my determination.

"I must go myself," I said. "Rehmah, see to the preparations for the journey. I must meet the king of Israel. I must meet Solomon."

I did not wait for his reply, but made my way from the throne room, confident that my orders would be carried out. It would take considerable planning and many weeks of organized application to complete our preparations for the long journey. It was to be among the grandest journeys in the annals of Sabaean history.

I could not rest until I met this most celebrated man on earth. "Could a man of such wealth also possess such profound wisdom?" I speculated. I have always sought the greatest wealth one can realize—wisdom! If even one-half of what I heard about King Solomon was true—his lofty riches, his palace of untold magnificence housing the most elaborate furnishings, and a mind containing untold wisdom—what a treasure he would be to know. I must meet him!

The recognition and acclaim of Solomon, even more than all his riches, is that he is known to be a man endowed with great wisdom—the greatest wealth of all! He is known to have said, "He who trusts in his own heart is a fool, but whoever walks wisely will be delivered."[2] And have you heard this pearl of wisdom? "There is gold and a multitude of rubies, but the lips of knowledge are a precious jewel."[3] Ahh, such wisdom is to be desired far above rubies!

The preparations continued at what seemed a snail's pace. My desire to be on my way was heightened even further when I met with an august group of my advisers.

Rehmah was the spokesman for the counselors. He stepped forward, a little apart from the rest as he said, "Kings from every nation, large and small, have sent their ambassadors to sit at the feet of this learned monarch. We have conferred and humbly suggest and urge that you do the same."

"I am surprised, Rehmah," I said. "Surprised that you understand me no better than that. No, I am determined that I must go myself. Whatever the cost—whatever the danger, I must go! I have to see for myself! I have to hear for myself!"

For you see . . . Far above rubies, silver or gold,
Wisdom's the treasure, with measure untold.
With heart, oh so bold, in dangers untold;
Wisdom o'er rubies, silver, or gold.

How far must we travel, what hazards we'll meet,
Our caravan moving o'er mountain and stream.
But onward we traverse, to wisdom's great store.
I'll see for myself wisdom's treasures galore.

Nothing can stop us, our mission prevails.
I must know the truth about all of the tales;
Solomon's riches, his wealth, wisdom too,
Can all this be real? I must know if it's true!

At last, the day of departure! There was great fanfare as we began our journey to wisdom. My aides helped me mount my jewel-studded camel. It was draped with the finest linen blankets to afford me some small measure of comfort as we made our way to the land beyond the mountains. My subjects lined the way as far as the eye could see. The musicians filled the air with their melodious songs depicting our triumphant Sabaean history. Our journey began. The music continued until we were out of earshot, but the melodies played in my head and cheered me during the long, tedious months of travel.

The journey was even more rigorous than I had imagined! "It will all be worth it," I told myself as I anticipated my audience with the renowned King Solomon. We traveled twelve hundred miles by way of the Trade Routes, roads that we Sabaeans control. We made our weary way through the Arabian Desert and across the land of Moab to the hills of Gilead.

Our long and winding caravan was an enormous opulent train making its way westward. We carried countless gifts of untold wealth to be presented to King Solomon. We needed an army to protect these treasures. I felt that I, too, was secure in their presence. My very finest military men—rivaled only by King David's Valiant Men— were ready for anything.

"This has been a good day," I said to my handmaiden at the end of yet another day's journey.

"Oh, yes, Majesty," she agreed as she helped me from my camel. "I heard reports from the caravan leader that we were able to travel almost twenty miles today!"

"A good day, indeed!" I laughed.

I took advantage of the long trip to frame the questions I would put to this celebrated man. I needed to see if he was as brilliant as he was reported to be. I thought of questions such as, "If two women came to you, both claiming to be the mother of the same child, how would you decide?"[4] "How will Solomon deal with that problem?" I wondered.

Finally, after long months of travel, the walls of Jerusalem came into view, nestled against a mountain. What a strategic position! Jerusalem, set like a priceless gem among jewels. In all of Israel, there was no greater city!

"Look," I said as I marveled at its glittering splendor. "Beautiful in elevation, the joy of the whole earth, is Mount Zion on the sides of the north, the city of the great King."[5]

We entered the city through the Golden Gate, escorted by Solomon's royal guards.

"You must see the Lord God's temple," our beautifully groomed escort advised. We followed him the short distance from the gate to the magnificent temple of Israel's God.

"Breathtaking!" I exclaimed. Its splendor defies description! With its cypress and cedar wood of Lebanon, and its magnificent stonework, the temple stood as a home fit for a God!

"Look, Rehmah!" I said, marveling at such graceful beauty. "What can one say about such elegance? What have you learned of that wonderful structure?"

His gaze followed mine as he related, "I heard, Majesty, that it required more than 183,000 men more than four years to complete construction of that noble temple!"

"That is correct," agreed our escort.

"What a temple!" I cried in delight. "What a city, Zion!"

Glorious things of thee are spoken, Zion, City of Yahweh.
On to wondrous men of glory, trusting now in what they say.
Solomon in all his splendor, beckons all from far and near;
Gifts and honor to him render, set before the king with cheer.

We approach with great desire, to behold the mighty throne;
Of beauty and of marvelous splendor,
    grace the world has yet not known.
Feast your eyes on Zion's City, every tittle, every jot;
To inspire such glorious passion, Yahweh must be Almighty God!

We turned our feet and our attention to the royal home. There was no more magnificent palace complex anywhere. It contained a series of five structures, including the anteroom for the throne where I would have audience with the king on the following day.

"King Solomon meets his most distinguished guests there," he told me.

Like a young maiden, I felt the thrill of anticipation as I prepared for my audience with King Solomon in his royal palace. The quarters provided for me were everything a queen could desire, from the blue curtains adorning the walls, to the tapestried couches for one's greatest comfort.

"I want my finest gown," I told Keziah, my handmaiden, as I prepared to bathe for my reception with the king. She knew exactly which one I had in mind. I did not linger in my bath, but hurried with the other preparations for my first meeting with the wisest man in all the earth. Finally, my hair properly plaited, my cosmetics carefully applied, I felt that I had done all that I could to impress Solomon with my beauty. All that remained was to impress him with my wisdom.

Everything I had endured was forgotten as I was ceremoniously ushered into the presence of the man whose wisdom is known and honored throughout the world. This was the moment to match his wits with mine—to gain from his wisdom and knowledge, even as I shared mine.

I trembled a bit as I approached his ornate throne. What a handsome man! I had heard that his father, King David, was "ruddy, and handsome, with pleasant eyes."[6] How like his father, I thought. As I drew nearer, Solomon rose from his throne. I was touched by the sincere gesture of respect, acknowledging my royal standing.

"Your Highness," he addressed me, bowing low in deference to my station.

"Your Majesty," I responded, matching his tone and demeanor. I marveled at the steadiness of my voice.

He seemed to flow down the three steps from his platform to greet me. The king took my trembling hand in his, and gently, oh, so gently, led me through a door that opened to the most magnificent throne room I had ever seen or even imagined. I felt the gasp of amazement escape my lips. How could one man or nation devise such beauty and splendor, I wondered. Every wall was ornately carved by gifted craftsmen. But the thing that dominated everything in the room was King Solomon's throne, which was made of carved ivory and inlaid with gold. He led me up the steps to the seat he had provided for me. We began our long-awaited discourse by exchanging royal pleasantries.

"How do you find our fair land, Israel?"

"Unique, and beautiful."

"Was your journey arduous?"

"Somewhat, but worthwhile," I admitted.

"Have you seen the vineyards and orchards?"

"Not yet, Majesty, but I look forward eagerly to that pleasure."

"And when you do," he added, "be sure to see the gardens as well."

Our conversation continued in that vein for some time before it took a more serious tone. I have no idea how long we sat in the splendor of his throne room discussing everything from pomegranates to positions of authority. Finally, our conversation turned to meatier topics, and the questions began. Now that I was more relaxed in the scintillating presence of one of the most articulate and powerful men in the world, I recalled some of the questions I had formed on the long journey to Israel.

"What if," I began, "what if a child is left to his own devices?"

Without hesitation, Solomon answered. "To discipline and reprimand a child produces wisdom, but a mother is disgraced by an undisciplined child."[7]

"What is the wisdom of searching for good?" I asked him.

"If you search for good," he said, "you will find favor. But, if you search for evil, it will find you."[8]

"If it please you, Majesty, could I ask another question?"

"Please do," he replied graciously.

"Does a king or queen need advisers?"

"By all means," he said. "Without wise leadership, a nation falls; with many counselors, there is safety."[9]

The questions continued in that vein until the evening shadows lengthened. Overwhelmed by the king's great wisdom, I said at last, "Oh, King Solomon, I have suffered much for this opportunity. I need to tell you, in all modesty, that I simply had to meet you. I had to see and hear for myself if all the things I heard about you were true. They were true—and more! What I heard was not the half of who and what you are.

"I was curious, my lord, but it was not merely idle curiosity. No. I had a burning desire to see your accomplishments, to hear your deep and profound wisdom—the wisdom the gods have given you."

"No, my dear lady," Solomon said in all seriousness. "Not the wisdom of the gods, but rather the wisdom of the God, Yahweh, the one, true God—the Almighty God. He said he would grant me whatever I requested. I asked for wisdom. God granted my request for wisdom and gave me riches as well."

The fervor in his voice as he spoke of his God quickened my heart. I caught the vision of his passion. My heart overflowed with its warmth.

I told the monarch, "It was true, King Solomon, it was true, what I heard in my own land about your words and your wisdom. But, Solomon, I did not believe those words until I saw it with my own eyes. Your wisdom and prosperity exceed their fame. Happy are your men and happy are your servants, who stand continually before you and hear your wisdom!

"Blessed be the Lord your God, who delighted in you, setting you on the throne of Israel! Because the Lord has loved Israel forever, therefore he made you king to do justice and righteousness."[10]

"**My heart overflows** with a beautiful thought! I will recite a lovely poem to the king, for my tongue is like the pen of a skillful poet.

> You are the most handsome of all.
> Gracious words stream from your lips.
> God Himself has blessed you forever."[11]

Only God could create such passion, that passion shared by two wisdom seekers. My passion deepened as I recalled the stories I had heard of this same God who had told Abraham that because of his seed all the nations of the earth would be blessed. And now I know that blessing has come to David and to Solomon, but, even beyond that, God's promise of blessing is for all people!

The lanterns were lighted and blazed with glory in the great throne room. With a great flourish, I commanded my slaves to bring all the treasure that I had brought with me from Sheba. First came the gold, in greater abundance than Israel had ever known, laden on linen pillows to display its beauty and brilliance. The slaves bearing the gold lined the walls of the ornate throne room, adding to its brilliant luster.

Rehmah gave the command, "Bring the spices we carried from our land to grace the courts of Solomon!" The sealed jars, all beautifully sculpted and colored, were carefully displayed as they were carried into the room.

"Open this one," I ordered. As the seal was broken on the blue jar of spikenard, the room was filled with its tantalizing fragrance. Never before had there been spices as fine as those that I presented to Solomon.

Finally the magnificent chests bearing the countless precious stones were presented to the king. Now at last, the courtroom was filled to overflowing with the lavish gifts that I, the Queen of Sheba, had brought to honor Solomon, the King of Israel and the bearer of great wisdom.

"How gracious, how generous you are," he said. He was clearly pleased by my gifts and by the esteem they signified.

"Please, dear lady," he added, "Tell me your heart's desire. I withhold nothing from you."[12]

I was overwhelmed with the emotion of the moment and the offer from so eminent a king who had already given me gifts according to my royal station. My gifts paled when compared to the blessing I had received from meeting King Solomon. Yet, such a noble offer was not to be refused. I accepted his majestic gift and returned to Sheba, changed forever.

> You ask me now, "What was the gift?
> Was it more than one, pray tell?"
> First of the gifts was knowledge of
> The Great God of Israel.

> Add to the treasures—another gift!
> Solomon hoped I would accept it.
> A gift of enormous consequence,
> But would it be rejected?

> Tell, I won't, though you may press,
> For answers sweet and mild.
> I know all the rumors. You may, too.
> Was his gift that of a child?

> We loved each other, respected, too,
> This much I will confess.
> That's all that I can tell you.
> The rest you'll have to guess.[13]

Has the quest for wisdom overtaken you? James 1 tells us that if you seek wisdom, " . . . ask God, and he will give it liberally, and without reproach." Proverbs 1:7 says, "The fear of the Lord is the beginning of knowledge, but fools despise wisdom and instruction" (NKJV).

Don't be a fool; seek wisdom. And trust God who is Wisdom and who gives it liberally. You just need to ask.

NOTES

1. Proverbs 8:14–16. (Unless otherwise indicated, Scriptures quoted in this chapter are from the New Living Translation of the Bible.)

2. Proverbs 28:26, NKJV.

3. Proverbs 20:15, NKJV.

4. 1 Kings 3:16–17, paraphrased.

5. Psalm 48:2, NKJV.

6. 1 Samuel 16:12.

7. Proverbs 29:15.

8. Proverbs 11:27.

9. Proverbs 11:14.

10. 1 Kings 10:9, NKJV.

11. Psalms 45:1,2.

12. 1 Kings 10:13, paraphrased.

13. According to legend, King Solomon and the Queen of Sheba had a love affair, purportedly resulting in a son named Menelek.

CHAPTER 5

Gomer

Sinner Restored

Money flows freely in Israel since Jeroboam II became king. I hear that it's the same down south in Judah, but I never get down there. Oh no, I'm stuck here in Bethel[1] since my family's all dead. I guess you'd say they're resting in the bosom of their fathers. I don't know about that. I just know they're dead, and when they died, so did any chance I might have to lead what you'd call a "respectable life."

As you might guess, they didn't leave many shekels, and being a single girl, I knew what I had to do. So I put on the only decent robe I had and went down to the local brothel. That was the beginning of my career. I'm Gomer, the daughter of Diblaim. Father's name meant "grape cakes," so from the time I was born, I was known as "the daughter of sensuality."

As a child I worshiped Yahweh God. But when I got a little older I became more interested in other gods, mainly Baal, Canaan's most important god. Everybody was doing it, so it must be okay, right? Besides, you could see Baal, well at least a wooden image of him. And you could take part in the sacrifices in the high places by the sacred poles.

This story takes approximately thirty minutes to present orally.
For more ideas, see "Hints for Presenters" at the beginning of this book.

But there was this one fellow, a prophet I think you would call him. Well, this prophet was the son of Beeri, and his name was Hosea. Have you heard of him?

Anyway, this prophet, Hosea, was always ripping into the people for worshiping any god if it wasn't Yahweh. And he would really tear into us for having golden calves in our sanctuaries at Bethel and Dan. He had plenty to say, too, about how the rich were getting richer and the poor were getting poorer. I guess I'd agree with that. I hardly ever had more than two coins in my pouch at the same time.

He was a farmer,[2] but people say that God talked to him. Then he'd come around to tell us what God said to him. I heard Hosea myself, and it wasn't pleasant I tell you. Have you ever heard anyone say, "Hear the word of the Lord, you children of Israel, for the Lord brings a charge against the inhabitants of the land, 'There is no truth or mercy or knowledge of God in the land. By swearing and lying, killing and stealing and committing adultery, they break all restraint, with bloodshed upon bloodshed'?"[3]

Ears perked up and so did tempers when he'd say things like, "You're going to waste away."

Then there was the day he came to Bethel. You can imagine my surprise when he talked to me. It seemed pretty clear to me that he had been looking for me. I just didn't know why.

"God has spoken to me," he said.

"Yeah," I said, "so I've heard."

"You don't understand," he explained. "God told me to come and get you."

"Get me?" Now I was really stunned! "What for?"

"Gomer," he went on, "you are to be my wife."

"I never knew you were a man of humor," I laughed. I couldn't help it. I laughed till I couldn't see for all the tears.

"I am serious, Gomer," he said. I noticed he wasn't laughing.

"I have no family," I told him. "I have no dowry."

"I know," he said. "I will provide the circlet of coins to adorn your head dress."[4]

I was dumbfounded. I couldn't say anything. I knew Hosea was serious, but for the life of me, I could not figure out why he wanted me for his wife.

I had no father, or even an uncle, who could say the formal words of betrothal to Hosea, "You are to be my son-in-law." Thus, as soon as my circlet of coins was fastened to my head dress, Hosea took me to be his bride. We did not wait the traditional year of betrothal. It was not the wedding I dreamed of. Actually, I didn't think anyone would ever marry me. I guess I should have been grateful to Hosea. It was obvious how much he loved me. That was a new experience—and so was farm life.

I thought my former "occupation" was hard, but farming had its own set of troubles. I'm glad Hosea did the plowing. But reaping and winnowing are no laughing matters either—up before the sun and work until you thought you would drop. Even during my pregnancy, it didn't let up.

But Hosea's a good man, actually the best I'd ever known! He tried to make things easier for me. Sometimes I'd look up from a task to see him looking at me with those big cow eyes. I didn't know how to take that. No one ever looked at me like that before. No one ever seemed to care!

And then, our baby boy was born. "Why did you name him Jezreel?" I demanded of Hosea.

"The lad is named for the valley where King Jehu carried out his bloody coup," he told me. It still didn't make sense. He saw the "I don't understand" look on my face.

"God scatters," he said, leaving the house to let me know there would be no more questions and, more to the point, no more answers.

Restlessness set in then, like a dark cloud. It overshadowed everything. I didn't particularly enjoy being a mother. In my world, a woman without children was incomplete, but I felt like there should be more to life. So when an old "acquaintance" showed up at the farm, we started spending time together. It was easy to get away with our visits because Hosea was away so often. He traveled all over Israel, telling people things like, "Israel is stubborn like a stubborn calf. Now the Lord will let them forage like a lamb in open country."[5] Maybe other people knew what he meant, but I had no idea what he was talking about.

Then the inevitable happened. I became pregnant again. Would Hosea suspect that the baby might not be his? I wondered. But he loved me so much that I didn't spend much time worrying about it. Life went on as usual, and then Lo-Ruhamah was born. My little girl was cursed with the name that means "not pitied."

"Why?" I screamed at Hosea. "Why would you give this child such an awful name?"

"God commanded it," he said. "Yahweh said, ' . . . I will no longer have mercy on the house of Israel, but I will utterly take them away.'"[6]

Before long I was back in the fields, reaping the grain. "Why is it such a plentiful crop this year?" I complained. Lo-Ruhamah was strapped to my back, while Jezreel toddled along behind me, batting at an occasional butterfly. Even his little-boy laughter did not raise my spirits. I felt a burning restlessness. Did you ever notice that the thing you don't have is the thing you want? Well, that was me. When life on the farm got hard, I would think about my old life. "Fantasize," I think you'd call it. At least that's what Hosea said whenever he saw what he called "that old look" in my eyes.

Well, my fantasizing kept on until I found ways to steal away from the dreary farm and go into Bethel to see my old friends. "Well, look who's back!" they would call out. They always seemed glad to see me. Why not? I was fun to be with. We'd spend hours talking and laughing—and flirting. It was the flirting that got me into trouble again.

One day some months later, I said to my little ones, "Uh oh, you're going to have a little brother or sister." They were delighted. I was woeful. Hosea seemed resigned. I'm sure he knew that I'd been up to my old tricks, spending time away from home while he was gone. He knew where I would go on my little jaunts.

This time the word he spoke from the Lord was directed at me, "Harlotry, wine and new wine enslave the heart."[7]

Then when the labor began, Hosea sent for the midwife. He didn't stay to console me in my anguish. He left, probably to talk things over with Yahweh. I saw the hurt in his eyes as he made his way past me and through the open door. By the time he got home, my son had been born. He had already been rubbed with salt and wrapped in cloths.

"His name shall be Lo-Ammi," Hosea announced. This time I did not even question him about why he chose such a strange name for my baby.

"The Lord has said, ' . . . you are not my people, and I will not be your God.'"[8]

"Oh, Hosea," I cried. "We are abandoned by Yahweh."

"No!" he insisted. "The Lord has said,

> . . . it shall come to pass in Jezreel, the very place where it was said to them, "You are not my people," there it shall be said to them, "you are the sons of the living God." Then Judah and Israel shall be returned

from Exile, reunited. They shall appoint for themselves one head; and they shall come up out of the land, for great will be the day of Jezreel, now transformed! Say to your brothers, "My people," and to your sisters, "Mercy is shown."

"What a day that will be—the day when God will sow his people in the fertile soil of their own land again!"[9]

"This is hard to believe, Hosea," I said. "Do you mean that Israel will someday be reunited with Judah, and we will once again be loyal only to Yahweh?"

"Yes," he said, "and in that day Yahweh will show us mercy."

I tried to understand it all, but it was too much for me. I just wasn't ready for such lofty thoughts. Besides, things weren't getting any better. I don't know what was worse—Hosea's relentless love, the hurt I saw in his eyes, or my restless loneliness. Yes, even with three children and all the farm work, I was lonely—lonely for my old friends, for the laughter, the wine, the songs. It wasn't long before I was slipping away again when Hosea was gone, but he knew. He knew.

Finally, the blow came. I guess I knew it would, it must. Hosea was in a rage when he got back from Samaria. "I've been up there in that sin-sick place," he accused, "while you've been here, committing sins of your own!"

I'll never forget the look in his eyes when he said to my children, "Bring charges against your mother, bring charges; for she is not my wife, nor am I her husband! Let her put away her harlotries from her sight; and her adulteries from between her breasts, lest I strip her naked and expose her, as in the day she was born, and make her like a wilderness, and set her like a dry land, and slay her with thirst!"[10]

I was in agony. "No, Hosea!" I cried in despair. "You can't divorce me! What shall I do? Where can I go?"

"Go back to your lovers!" he said and brushed past me, more angry than I had ever seen him.

Tears of frustration blinded me. "I never thought it would come to this," I thought as I gathered my things. I had no choice. With those words, "She is not my wife, nor am I her husband," the divorce was complete. The marriage was over. There was nothing I could do.

"Where are you going?" the children asked, clinging to me.

"He has divorced me," I screeched, trying to shake them off. "He wants me out of here, out of his life."

"Can't we come too?" Lo-Ruhamah asked.

I pictured my daughter in the brothel. "No! No way!" I said. I pushed her away, and she fell against Lo-Ammi with such force that they both fell flat on their bottoms. Before they could get up, I was out the door and on my way.

The way seemed long to Bethel. I was angry. Then I was sad. Then I was relieved to be getting away from the awful routine of farm life and the drag of being a wife and mother. Then I was angry again. "Who does Hosea think he is, anyway?" my rebellious heart demanded.

"But he did love me!" some part of me responded. I kept trudging on, toward Bethel and my old life. "Hold your head high!" I reminded myself. "Besides, I'm going back where I belong." And then—I was there.

I laughed with my friends at the thought of my divorce. But if the truth were known, I didn't feel like it. Now I was back where I started. The realization stuck me that I needed to earn my own way to keep myself from starving, or worse. And, I wasn't sixteen anymore. I was kidding myself if I thought I was just as desirable as I had been before I was married and had borne three children.

I couldn't forget Hosea's parting words, "Now I will uncover her lewdness in the sight of her lovers, and no one shall deliver her from my hand. I will also cause all her mirth to cease, her feast days, her New Moons, her Sabbaths—all her appointed feasts. And I will destroy her vines and her fig trees, of which she has said, 'These are my rewards that my lovers have given me.' So I will make them a forest, and the beasts of the field shall eat them. I will punish her for the days of the Baals to which she burned incense. She decked herself with her earrings and jewelry, and went after her lovers. Then she forgot me."[11]

Strange—sometimes I thought he was talking about me, and sometimes it seemed like a prophecy for Israel. Could it be both? Whichever it was, it was scary.

But one thing was certain: I did deck myself out with my earrings and jewelry. And I did go after my lovers. And I did forget Hosea. Who does he think he is, anyway?

It wasn't very long before I ran out of lovers—and friends. Have you ever been alone? I mean, totally alone? I had been one of the most sought-after women in the brothel. Yes, I was. But not any more. Only Jonodab still came around. I didn't even like him. He wasn't all that crazy about me either. But he was the only one left.

"Jonodab," I said one day in my most alluring way. I could hardly keep from getting sick when he looked at me. His eyes were always moist and colorless. His nose was red like the flowers on a bramble bush. His hands were flabby and white, like the rest of him—and his breath!—like sulfur! Ugh.

"What is it, Raisin Cake?" he asked in his toneless voice.

"We've always been good together, haven't we?" I asked. I knew I was opening a door that would be very hard to close, but I was desperate.

He was suspicious. "I guess so," he said.

"Well," I said, "I was just thinking. We could come to some sort of arrangement."

"Oh?" he said. I could tell he was wondering what was in it for him.

"I've been around a while," I said.

"I'll say!" he laughed.

This was getting harder, but I went on. "Jonodab," I said, trying to sound like I really cared about the pig. "I think it's time for me to settle down."

"You tried that before," he laughed, "with that old prophet, Hosea. I don't think I'm ready to deal with that."

"Oh, but you don't understand," I cooed. "I would belong to you, and to none other." I took a deep breath. Finally I made myself look into those watery eyes and pretend I really cared for the swine. "Jonodab, I'm proposing to sell myself to you—to be your slave." There, I said it. It was repulsive, but I had no choice. All other doors had been closed to me, and if Jonodab refused me, I'd be lost.

He looked at me for a long time. "You're not worth much," he said scornfully. I swallowed hard, and didn't say anything. But I thought something, "You're worth even less!"

"What are you asking?" he said.

He was considering it! I was so relieved that I blurted out, "Anything. Nothing. Whatever you think right."

"You drive a hard bargain," he said, laughing till the tears ran down his fat cheeks. I could hardly keep from reaching out and tearing out his eyes. But I kept my peace. I did nothing. I said nothing. I lowered my head in a sign of submission. He grabbed my arm so roughly that my skin burned beneath his grip.

Life had been hard before. Now it became unbearable, impossible. Jonodab was a beast. He used me. He abused me.

I looked back at my years with Hosea with fresh eyes. The eyes of repentance. The eyes of regret. Would Hosea ever look upon me with eyes of forgiveness? How could he? I had played the harlot, as he would say. And he was right. Tears were my constant companion as one weary day slipped into another. The youthful luster was gone. The fun, the laughter, the wine, the lovers—all were a distant, fading memory. Each day the longing grew stronger, the longing for the comfort of the one man who had truly loved me—Hosea.

His words came to me, words of prophecy for Israel, but words that were meant for me too: "My God will cast them away, because they did not obey him; and they shall be wanderers among the nations."[12] "You have plowed wickedness; you have reaped iniquity. You have eaten the fruit of lies, because you trusted in your own way . . ."[13]

And then, one day, Jonodab came storming toward me as I was washing clothes by the stream. He was moving more quickly than usual, his thick body shaking beneath his faded robe.

"Come," he ordered. "I have a buyer."

He grabbed my arm roughly, as had become his habit. He pulled me to my feet saying, "Come on, woman! Don't be so slow. I don't want to lose this customer."

He wore his usual smirk as he pulled me along, up the dusty path toward his hut. He called it "home," but I never could. As we neared the hovel, I saw the customer. He was standing beside the open door, straight and tall. "It can't be!" I thought when I saw who it was.

"Hosea!" I called out. "Is it really you?"

"Quiet, woman!" Jonodab ordered. He jerked my arm to protest my audacity. "How dare you speak, slave!" he said between clenched teeth. Oh, how I loathed that wretched man! But I lowered my head in submission to my master.

"Shalom, Hosea," he greeted cheerily. "Ready to do business?"

At first Hosea said nothing. I raised my eyes and looked full in his face. There were tears in his eyes. I wanted to run to the comfort of his embrace, but Jonodab still clutched my arm.

"Yes, I'm ready," Hosea said, omitting the greeting of shalom. "What is your price?"

"Fifteen shekels of silver," Jonodab said. "And, oh yes, one and one-half homers of barley.[14] Small price to pay for a slave, even this 'used' one," he said, spitting out the words in his hateful way.

"The Lord has spoken," Hosea said. "He said, 'Hosea, fall in love with an unfaithful woman who has a lover. Do this to show that I love the people of Israel, even though they worship idols and enjoy the offering cakes made with fruit.'[15]

"Here is the payment, Jonodab," Hosea said. His tone was cold. Jonodab released his grip on my arm and took the payment from Hosea. His movement was so abrupt that I fell to the ground. Hosea helped me to my feet. His touch was gentle. It gave me a feeling of calm, of peace, of going home.

"Blessed are you, Hosea. Please, can we go home? My only desire is to be with you back on the farm," I said.

Still unsmiling, he mounted his little donkey.[16] "Yes," he said, looking down at my upturned face. "Sow for yourself righteousness; reap in mercy; break up your fallow ground, for it is time to seek the Lord, till he comes and rains righteousness on you."[17]

And with that, we began our homeward journey.

Things become different when you become different. I had changed. I was different—a different person. From the very start, I knew that Hosea loved me. And because he first loved me, I love him. I was an adulterous wife, running after false lovers—just like Israel and the false gods of Canaan. Those lovers could never love me the way Hosea does. Now when Hosea prophesies, I know that Yahweh God uses him and me to mirror the Lord and Israel.

I thrill to the words God speaks through his prophet and my husband, Hosea:

> I will heal their backsliding, I will love them freely, for my anger has turned away from him. I will be like the dew to Israel; he shall grow like the lily, and lengthen his roots like Lebanon. His branches shall spread; his beauty shall be like an olive tree, and his fragrance like Lebanon. Those who dwell under his shadow shall return; they shall be revived like grain, and grow like the vine. Their scent shall be like the wine of Lebanon. Ephraim shall say; "What have I to do anymore with idols?" I have heard and observed him. I am like a green cypress tree; your fruit is found in me.[18]

The restlessness is gone. I have found my shalom in the one true God, the God who loves, the God who forgives, the God who restores. Thank you, Lord!

The story in the Book of Hosea is like a mirror—Hosea's love and forgiveness for Gomer reflects God's love and forgiveness for the people of Israel. God commanded Hosea to marry Gomer to give the people of Israel a "visual aid." I thank the Lord whose love has an incomparable depth that could only be divine. God expresses this love in Hosea's eleventh chapter:

When Israel was a child, I loved him,
And out of Egypt I called my son.
As they called them; so they went from them,
They sacrificed to the Baals,
    and burned incense to carved images.
I taught Ephraim to walk, taking them by their arms;
But they did not know that I healed them.
I drew them with gentle cords, with bands of love.
And I was to them as those who take the yoke from their neck.
I stooped and fed them . . .
How can I give you up, O Ephraim?
How can I hand you over, O Israel? . . .
My heart churns within me; my sympathy is stirred.[19]

Thank you Lord, for the ultimate visual aid of your love as seen in your son, our Savior, Jesus Christ, who loves us and gave himself for us.

NOTES

1. The Bible doesn't tell us where Gomer lived. Since Hosea spoke of the city, condemning it for being not the House of God, but rather the House of Wickedness (Beth Aven), perhaps that is where Gomer herself resided.

2. Hosea's extensive knowledge of animals, both domestic and wild, plus his understanding of farm life indicates that he may indeed have been a farmer, even though the Bible doesn't tell us.

3. Hosea 4:1–2. (Unless otherwise indicated, Scriptures quoted in this chapter are from the New King James Version of the Bible.)

4. The circlet of coins, which was worn as a headdress, was equivalent to the modern-day wedding ring.

5. Hosea 4:16.

6. Hosea 1:6.

7. Hosea 4:11.

8. Hosea 1:9.

9. Hosea 1:10b–11, paraphrased.

10. Hosea 2:2-3.

11. Hosea 2:10–13.

12. Hosea 9:17.

13. Hosea 10:13.

14. Silver shekel = 1/2 oz. silver; Homer = 2+ dry pints; the fifteen shekels of silver and 1 1/2 homers was quite an insignificant price to pay for a slave. Gomer's value had greatly decreased.

15. Hosea 3:1, CEV. Offering cakes made with fruit, also described as raisin cakes, were used in idol worship.

16. The custom of that time was for the man to ride the animal and for the woman to walk.

17. Hosea 10:12.

18. Hosea 14:4–8.

19. Hosea 11:1–4,8.

Esther

For a Moment Such as This

In the golden sunset and the brilliant sunrise, I am reminded of the wondrous palace in Persia's beautiful city, Susa. That is where King Xerxes[1] crowned me, a Jewish maiden, to be his queen—Queen Esther—to share the beauty and splendor of the royal palace.

How can I describe such sublime loveliness? . . . the royal palace—adorned with white and blue curtains, fastened with cords of fine linen and purple and silver rods . . . the pillars—priceless marble . . . the couches—gold and silver resting on a mosaic pavement of alabaster, turquoise, white and black marble.

Life is not simple, even for a queen—perhaps most of all for a queen. The choices we must make can be life-changing, even life-threatening. But Yahweh God is with those who love him. He is the God of miracles and wisdom. It was God who imparted such wisdom to my dear uncle, Mordecai, wisdom that Mordecai shared with me, his adopted daughter.

I sing of that wisdom . . .

This story takes approximately forty-five minutes to present orally.

Including distribution and use of the noisemakers for the Purim tradition will add an additional five minutes.

For more ideas and an explanation of the Purim, see "Hints to Presenters" at the beginning of this book.

Far above rubies, silver, or gold,
Wisdom's the treasure, with measure untold.
Greatly displayed in gallantry bold.
Wisdom's o'er rubies, silver, or gold!

Mordecai wisely advised me, "Be bold!"
With prayer and with fasting the story unfolds;
Save God's chosen people from horror untold.
Wisdom and courage o'er silver and gold.

So you see:
Far above rubies, silver, or gold,
Wisdom's the treasure, with measure untold.

King Xerxes' reputation for his ostentatious celebrations was well founded. The smallest excuse was all he needed to send out the invitations. Before I became queen, King Xerxes hosted one of his famous opulent parties. Everyone of importance was invited. It was an invitation one could not refuse. No one did. Xerxes was ecstatic. For fully one half year the supercilious king entertained his guests. It gave him untold pleasure to show them the magnificent riches of Persia's glorious kingdom and the splendor of his own excellent majesty.

Then, as the six months were drawing to a close, he hosted a final decadent feast—one that lasted for seven days! The king wanted to be remembered for his elaborate parties, and there is no doubt that he would be. It is well known that the final feast of the kingdom's most celebrated party was the pinnacle of decadence and debauchery. Simply said, the king and his guests partook of too much food and too much drink. While all this reveling was taking place, Xerxes' Queen Vashti hosted a party for the women.

On the seventh day of his party, King Xerxes sent for Queen Vashti. "Bring her here!" he commanded. "She must wear her crown. I want my guests to see my beautiful queen."

"Was the crown the only adornment Xerxes expected Vashti to be wearing?" I asked my adopted father, Mordecai. "Did the king expect his queen to appear before his drunken guests unveiled—or wearing nothing but her royal crown?"

"I don't know," was his sad reply. "But perhaps that is why Queen Vashti did the unthinkable."

"What did she do, Father?" I asked.

"She refused the king's order," he said, shaking his head from side to side. "The king was embarrassed to say the least—and furious. His advisors felt that something had to be done. 'After all,' they told the king, 'We do not want the women of our land becoming haughty, refusing to obey their husbands! No, they must be kept in their place!'² And Xerxes agreed."

"How dreadful," I countered. "Didn't Queen Vashti know that she might have to pay with her life?"

"She may have," Father replied. "I don't know. The king and his advisors decided that she should be banished, and the crown was stripped from her."

How I admired Vashti, and her decision! Whatever the consequences, she would not compromise. Hers was a moral choice of noble character.

Even though his harem was full of the most beautiful, the fairest women in all the land, King Xerxes was not content. "I need a queen!" he bellowed. He set about making plans for a beauty contest, perhaps the first the world had ever known. For two long years, his army roamed all of Persia, seeking the most beautiful maidens, girls from the countryside as well as the cities.

I shall never forget the day I was taken to the palace as a reluctant contestant. "Father," I said to Mordecai. "What will happen to me? We have never been apart. I need you."

"It's a fearful prospect," Father agreed. "But the king commanded his officers to find all the beautiful girls of the kingdom. He told his men not to miss any. 'Not even one!' is what he said."

Even as the soldiers waited for me, dear Mordecai held me in his strong embrace, and whispered gently, "Don't fear, Little Hadassah. Pray always. Remember who you are. Even though just a youth, you are one of God's chosen people. But," he warned, "don't, under any circumstances, tell anyone that you are a Jew." Yahweh God's wisdom of discretion filled my soul from that moment as I obeyed Mordecai's command of silence.

I spent a fearful year being prepared for my appearance before King Xerxes. It was difficult to enjoy the luxury of my beautiful suite and my seven handmaidens. I could not forget valiant Queen Vashti and her stand for virtue and morality. Could I be as courageous? I hoped so, but was not sure, not having been put to the test.

I was comforted to know that dear Mordecai came to the court of the woman's quarters every day. He needed to be reassured about my safety and well being, just as I needed the assurance that he was nearby. I was further comforted by the friendship of Hegai, the king's eunuch, who not only saw to my preparation prior to being presented to the king, but advised me to use discernment and wisdom when I would be called before him.

Finally the day for that appearance arrived. I trembled ever so slightly when I was brought into his presence. I was carefully attired in the finest blue linen. An array of precious jewels adorned my arms and ankles. An abundance of beautiful gems had been braided into my long ebony hair. My name had been changed from Hadassah to Esther, which has the same meaning as Ishtar, who is said to be the Persian goddess of love. The name seems appropriate because from the moment our eyes met, I felt Xerxes' passion for me.

I suffered a pang of discomfort as his gaze fixed on me for long moments. At last his thunderous voice broke the silence, "Esther! Make your requests of me!" The display of opulence before me was there for the asking, but I remembered the advice of Hegai, my court advisor, to request the simplest of things.

"Majesty," I began, bowing low before the throne. "Such beauty and grandeur is too noble for me. But, if you please, I would request only a small token of your kindness."

The silence was profound. "Have I blundered?" I speculated. Then in greatly subdued tones Xerxes said, "Esther, my fair goddess of love, I choose you, above all the other beautiful virgins, not only for your beauty, but for your profound wisdom as well."

As I had obtained grace and favor in his sight, the king himself set a royal crown upon my head. "Esther," he said with authority, "I hereby name you my queen." The court erupted with cheers of approval at his announcement. I merely smiled and allowed the crown to be placed upon my head.

A breathtaking coronation celebration followed! King Xerxes proclaimed a holiday in my name and gave generous gifts to one and all. Still Mordecai continued to urge me to keep my Jewish heritage a secret.

"Why, Father?" I asked. "Are we and our people not secure, now that I am queen?"

"No, no, my dear Hadassah," he whispered. "Enemies are all around. Why just today I overheard a scheme to kill King Xerxes."

"What?" I uttered in surprise.

"Oh yes," he said. "Bigthan and Teresh are plotting to slay the king at this very moment."

I was appalled. When Mordecai finished telling me all that he knew, I sent word to the king of the plot, and that it was Mordecai who had reported it to me. The two would-be assassins were quickly apprehended and executed. In reality, Mordecai saved Xerxes' life! How sweet of our Lord to provide this opportunity. Mordecai's report was one of the keys to salvation for himself and the other Jews in Persia because Mordecai had a formidable enemy—the depraved and abominable Haman.

I shudder at the thought of that venomous creature. I could never understand why the king gave so much power to such an evil man. Haman had a position of absolute authority. He gave orders that all people were expected to carry out. He even commanded that everyone in the kingdom bow before him as though he were deity.

"I won't do it!" Mordecai told me adamantly. "We worship Yahweh God, Hadassah. We can not bow before any idol—especially that oppressor, Haman!"

I trembled at the thought of what our enemy would do. He made no secret of his hatred for Father Mordecai, and toward all Jews for that matter. "What if he plots to kill us all?" I grieved.

I spent many restless days and sleepless nights as I considered the fate of my people. My imagination was filled with pictures of doom and despair, conjuring up the most hideous events one could envision. I knew that my husband, the king, was easily swayed by flattery and cunning arguments. Haman was capable of both, I was sure. I did not have long to wait to see the lengths to which this depraved brute would go to destroy his enemies, the Jews!

The first inkling of the horror was the news that my dear Father Mordecai was in deep mourning. "He is at the gate of the palace," Hathach, my eunuch, told me. "He is wearing sackcloth and has heaped ashes upon his head."

I sent Hathach with clothing for Mordecai, but when he returned, Hathach still had the garments. "He won't accept them," he told me. "He gave me this letter and said I must deliver it to you, and to no one else."

I took the note with trembling fingers. It was from my dear adoptive father, Mordecai, and brought somber tidings indeed.

"Hadassah," the letter began, "The news is not good. The worst will happen if we do not act quickly. Haman has succeeded. He has pressed the king to issue a decree. And, my dear, it is a dark day for us Jews! Here is a copy of that dreaded document:

"'It is decreed and commanded by Xerxes, King of Persia, that all Jews, male and female, young and old, including all women and little children, must be killed, annihilated in one day, on the thirteenth day of the twelfth month, which is the month of Adar. It is further decreed that all goods and properties belonging to the assassinated Jews is subject to plunder.'"

A chill of despair enveloped me as I continued reading. "The couriers have already gone out, Hadassah. Less than one year from now, all Jews are to be murdered."

I gasped, unbelieving. My mind could not take in such horror. All? My mind screamed in disbelief.

I went back to reading the epistle of doom. "Esther," he wrote, using the name given me by King Xerxes to signify my position, "you, Queen Esther, have it in your power to save your people."

"I have no power!" my heart protested. But I read on.

"Only you can save your people. You, Esther, must go before Xerxes to petition for the lives of the Jews."

I put the missive down and wrote a hurried note in response to my dear Mordecai.

"I can't do that! No one goes before the king unless invited. The law is clear—unless the king holds out his scepter to you, the penalty is death!"

Hathach was quick to bring the message to my mourning father. It seemed forever until his return. He came at last, bearing yet another message.

Mordecai's reply was chilling, "Do not think, Hadassah, that you will escape any more than all the other Jews! Do you think your heritage can be kept secret? And if you do not go to Xerxes, if you do remain silent, you can be sure that deliverance will rise up from other Jews, and you and your father's house will all perish. Yet, who knows—Queen Esther—you may have been born for such a time as this!"

The choice was before me. There was no escaping its implications. So I prayed and fasted, along with every other Jew in Persia. After the three days and nights of fasting were completed, I made my way with heavy heart to seek an audience with King Xerxes, resigned to the fact that if I perish, I perish.

The doors were thrown open for me as I approached the throne room. I looked neither to the left nor to the right, but kept my eyes on the king, seated on his royal throne. His gaze was steady and formidable. Those who had already been granted audience with the most powerful man in the world stared in disbelief as I made my way resolutely down the marbled hall. Each step brought me ever nearer to the man who held my life in his hands. But as I grew closer, a calm nurtured my soul. My heart rejoiced that Xerxes had no power but what had been granted by Yahweh God. The wisdom and courage God had granted me was for that very moment in my life. I watched breathlessly as Xerxes raised his sceptered hand. And then, unmistakably, the scepter pointed to me!

"What do you wish, Queen Esther? Whatever you desire, it shall be yours, up to half my kingdom."

"No, my lord," I said, greatly relieved. "If it please the king, only let the king and Haman come to the banquet I have prepared."

My request was granted, and while we feasted, Xerxes raised his wine glass and said, "Now Queen Esther, tell me—what would you really like me to do for you?"

"Oh, Majesty," I replied with all humility, "this is my request and my deepest desire. If your Majesty is pleased with me and wants to grant my request, please come with Haman tomorrow to the banquet I will prepare for you. Then, tomorrow, I will tell you what is on my heart."

Haman could not conceal his delight. He thought that he had found favor with me, and that it might enhance his position with the king. What he didn't know was that Mordecai, the man he hated most in all the world, was my adoptive father. I knew that our enemy had built a scaffold. He wanted to hang the one man who would not bow to him.

But Yahweh was in control and intervened. As preparations were being made for the banquet, I had a visit from Hegai, my most trusted advisor.

"Highness," he said, bowing low, "I have news of great import. News I feel will help you and your people."

"What is it?"

"His Majesty the king was restless and could not sleep last night," he said. "So he had my friend, Shaashgaz, the chamberlain, come to him in the courtyard with the book of records. King Xerxes told Shaashgaz to read it to him. In the course of his reading, he came upon the passage that spoke of Mordecai and his help in thwarting the plans of the would-be assassins. 'What?' King Xerxes demanded. 'Has no reward been given Mordecai for his loyalty?'"

Hegai went on to relate that at that precise moment a man entered the courtyard—it was none other than Haman! It was then I knew that Yahweh God was arranging everything and would save us from the evil plot of our vile enemy!

Hegai added, "The king asked Haman what he thought should be done for the man whom the king delights to honor."

What a sense of humor our Lord has! Haman must have thought that the king was speaking of him, because Hegai told me that he suggested to King Xerxes, "Bring one of the king's finest robes and the king's horse, the one wearing a royal crest upon his head. Then have a parade for the honored one, proclaiming, 'Behold, make way for the man whom the king delights to honor.'"

Hegai chuckled as he related the events. "The king was delighted, and he told your enemy, 'Hurry, take the robe and the horse as you have suggested, and you do this. Give this recognition to the man in whom I most delight—my faithful new chancellor, Mordecai.'"

My heart sang with joy. The wretched fool had no choice. There was nothing for him to do but to follow the king's orders. What humiliation he suffered—at his own evil hands!

I could see plainly on his face and in his demeanor that he was still in the throes of anguish when he and the king arrived for my banquet. I pretended not to notice as we took our places at the feast. The king seemed oblivious to Haman's discomfort. He was curious about my delayed request.

"All right, Queen Esther," he began. "You said that you would make your request known today. Now is the time." He was smiling, anticipating some girlish whim, I suppose.

My choice had been made. It was not a girlish whim. I felt the calm of the Lord as I said, "If I have found favor in your sight, O king, and if it pleases you, I beg of you, Lord, spare my life, and the lives of my people." The king's jaw dropped in shocked horror, but I continued. "For, O Majesty, we have all been sold to be murdered. Had we merely been sold as slaves, I would have held my tongue, although my Lord, the enemy could never compensate for the king's loss of all these loyal subjects."

I held my breath as King Xerxes' face reddened with rage. "Who is this enemy? Who would dare presume to do such a thing?"

There was no turning back. The prince of darkness was about to be exposed as I said in slow, steady tones, "The enemy and adversary, my king, is the wicked and evil—Haman!"

The king was outraged! He leaped from his chair in raging fury. "Seize that man!" he ordered, pointing a judicious finger at the doomed man of corruption. Haman's cries of protest, mingled with pleas for mercy, did not help, but only further infuriated King Xerxes. "You, Haman," he bellowed, "will hang this very day on the very gallows you built for my faithful Mordecai!" The defeated vermin was led sobbing from my chambers. I never saw him again.

The king made a complete turn-about in his orders regarding my people. He even decreed that the Jews be given every opportunity to defend themselves against the onslaught Haman had devised to destroy them.

Ah, but ultimately, the battle was the Lord's, and Yahweh was victorious.

Wisdom, and our perception of it, plays its part in all our decisions. Our Lord God, the giver of all good gifts, granted me wisdom to be obedient and courageous with the courage that only comes through faith. It is not merely wisdom that has a high degree of knowledge, but wisdom that has the power of true and right discernment, that is granted by our Lord.

Christ is the wisdom of God.[3] And that wisdom is granted to all who will accept, no matter what choices we may have made.

And God has a plan. We've all heard that—maybe so much that it no longer makes an impact on us. God is love. We've all heard that, too—maybe so much that it makes no impact on us either. But God IS love and God's plan for you, for me, is born out of that love. What is that plan? It is abundant, everlasting life.

For God so loved the world that He gave His only begotten Son that whoever believes in Him should not perish but have everlasting life.[4]

God's Plan (John 3:16)

God has a special plan for you, A plan for your very life;
One of peace and happiness, Ending inner strife.

For God so loved the world, He gave his only Son.
Believe in him—have eternal life, The battle has been won.

Sounds too simple to be true, You think there should be more.
You want to earn eternal life, Get your foot in heaven's door.

But it can't be by your efforts, Friend. Accept God's gift of grace.
Trust Jesus as your Savior. At the helm, he'll take his place.

Make Jesus Christ your pilot; He's the Way, the Truth, the Life.
Peace will be your standard, God's Word your guiding light.
    Amen.

NOTES

1. The biblical story of Esther can be found in the Book of Esther. The near-legendary figure of the Persian king is probably Xerxes I, who ruled from 486–465 B.C. Xerxes was the Greek form of his name, and so the New International Version and New Living Translation of the Bible render it. The King James tradition uses his Persian name, Ahasuerus.

2. Esther 1:13–20.

3. See 1 Corinthians 1:24.

4. John 3:16, NKJV.

Claudia Procula

Wife of the Scoundrel, Pontius Pilate

My name is Claudia Procula.[1] Mine is a proud name and proud heritage. My grandfather, Caesar Augustus, was the first Emperor of Rome. He wasn't always known as Augustus. No, he gave himself that illustrious name when he became the emperor. Before that his name was simply Octavian.

Did you know that he and Antony co-ruled Rome until civil war broke out? It was then that they found themselves on opposite sides of the conflict. It's a long story, so I won't go into all the details, but when Grandfather won, Antony and his ally, Cleopatra, committed suicide. Actually, that was not uncommon in those days. Losing had no valor and the most valid option was to end it all gloriously and thus be with the gods.

My father, Tiberias, succeeded Grandfather in the year A.D. 14. Father was an able ruler, resolute and just. And having high regard for the fortunes of the Empire as a whole, he was very successful. Yes, I am proud of my name and of my heritage.

Antipas, the second Herod of Israel, also held my father in high regard. He built a magnificent city. To honor Father, Herod gave it

---

The story takes approximately sixty minutes to present orally.
For more ideas, see "Hints for Presenters" at the beginning of this book.

Father's name, Tiberias. I had occasion to visit there recently. No cost was spared in the planning and creation of this magnificent city! It took nine long years to build, but it was worth every effort. The palace is adorned with an elegant gold roof. And you should see all the precious things that beautiful palace houses! There are sculptures and delicate pottery art objects from every part of the world. The couches, tables, draperies, all the furnishings are breathtaking, exquisite to the eye and to touch. I dare say its magnificence has no equal in that primitive part of the world!

The city is home for thirty-five thousand people, and the mammoth sports stadium holds ten thousand of them at one time! Isn't it incredible to realize that, even with all of its beauty and culture, many of the Jews who live there are not happy? They object simply because Tiberias was built on an ancient cemetery. These people are so quaint. I do try to understand them and to sympathize, but I must admit, I have not always been successful!

As I have said, I am proud of my name. But sadly, I am not so proud of my husband's. It's quite famous, or should I say, infamous? His name? Pontius Pilate. Have you heard of him? I would really be surprised if you have not. Pontius and I really cared for each other. He was quite tender—with me. I have no illusions, however. I know that my position in the Caesar family commands a great deal of respect, and part of his devotion and attention to me was due to that fact.

I was attracted to Pontius the very first time I saw him. I was just returning to the royal palace in Rome from the Temple of Diana. He was with a group of other young officers in the bustling outer courtyard of the palace. They appeared to be engaged in a serious discussion. My chariot driver slowed the pace to avoid running down the people who occupied the spacious enclosure.

"Who is that fellow?" I asked Julia, my companion nurse.

"Which fellow?" she responded, looking at the sea of young men surrounding our vehicle.

I told Julia that he was standing a little apart from the rest. "The one holding his javelin in his left hand," I said, pointing discreetly.

Julia scanned the scene, looking for a left-handed young man. The moments seemed an eternity until her eyes fell upon him. "Oh, I believe that is Pontius Pilate," she told me. I saw the look of curiosity in Julia's eyes, but she dared not question a princess, at least not verbally. And I dared not respond to her questioning eyes. We hurried on.

The next day—the very next day—I saw him again. He really is handsome—striking, I mused. My heart beat a little faster at the sight of him. Again, Pontius was with that same group of young men. I had overheard that they were in diplomatic training. I also learned that Pontius was the son of an eminent Roman family. He had already served some time in the military.

Later that afternoon I found the courage to speak to my father regarding Pontius. "Father," I asked, "how long do men have to be in diplomatic training?"

"What a strange question for you to ask, Claudia," he said with a smile. "Is there some diplomat in particular you are interested in?" The twinkle in his eye caught my attention. I felt my cheeks redden.

"Father!" I said in mock horror.

He laughed aloud then, pleased with his joke. "Pontius Pilate will be here for some time," he said. I had not fooled Father at all. Somehow he knew that my interest in diplomatic training had a more personal bent.

Father became a bit more serious then as he continued, "He's already had a few minor posts. We'd like to see if he's ready for something bigger. He shows some promise, and may make a satisfactory governor somewhere in the Empire. We shall see."

I never knew whether or not it had been Father who had arranged for the dinner party that took place several weeks later. It was an elaborate affair with jesters and jugglers, poets and dancers. The diplomatic students were there as well as other court dignitaries. It was at that event that Pontius' eyes and mine met in a moment of exquisite delight. Later, when it seemed prudent to do so, I wandered out onto the portico, hoping that Pontius would find a discreet way to follow. He did. And soon we were shyly exchanging pleasantries while getting acquainted. Julia remained a tactful distance away.

Our wedding was the social event of the year! Because I am the daughter of the emperor, dignitaries from around the world clamored for the opportunity to be on the guest list. My wedding gown was of the finest materials available and carefully beaded with precious jewels. Rome's finest beauticians carefully dressed my hair in the latest, most becoming fashion. Others artfully applied makeup to enhance my skin and eyes, radiant with joyful anticipation.

Ah, the sweet ecstasy of the occasion. My cup of bliss could not be contained. It overflowed in great splashes of sparkling mirth. I savored every moment of the weeklong event. And dear Pontius could hardly contain himself. He was beaming and elegant—the most handsome man in the world, I was sure—like a great cedar of Lebanon.

But then, for the first time, I saw a side of him that made me uneasy. When he realized that the wine had not been properly chilled, he lost his temper, berating the servant mercilessly. "You slavish, worthless fool!" he shouted. "Your worth is less than that of a torn sandal, ready for the dung heap. I'll have your hide for this!"

When Pontius saw my surprised displeasure he apologized. "Oh, Claudia, my darling, forgive me. I just want everything to be right—for you." The party continued without incident, but my heart was no longer light.

One afternoon, about eight months after our wedding, Pontius surprised me with the news we had been waiting for. "I've been given my appointment, Claudia," he announced.

"Oh Pontius, at last," I said. "Where are we going?"

"We?" he said. "Governors do not take their wives along."

"Governor!" I said. "Where? Where will they send you?"

He seemed a bit more subdued as he told me, "Judea."

"Judea?" I said, incredulous. "Pontius, you're too good for such a backward province." His face turned the color of blood as he fought to control his temper.

"Oh, my dear," I said, wanting to soothe his hurt feelings, "they could find no one better to govern those obstinate people. You're steady. And solid. You're resolute. Darling, no one stands more firm in their convictions than you. And, Pontius," I added brightly, "I'll go with you. I'll talk to Father now."

I dared not wait for his response. Without another word, I left the chamber, determined to have my way in this.

The journey from Rome to Judea was long and difficult. Our caravan left Rome in mid-April, when the spring breezes rustled in the budded trees that lined the Appian Way. We headed south, journeying to Three Taverns, our first checkpoint. It was good to stretch a bit before continuing to the Forum of Appius, perhaps the best-known way station on the Appian Way. We spent the night there and started out early the next morning, determined to accomplish the forty-three miles to the great commercial port at Puteoli.

"I'll be so glad," Pontius said as we boarded the ship, "so glad to get my sea legs and leave the land behind for a while!"

"Yes," I agreed, "and the ship's captain assured me that we can make much better time, too."

There was a lightness of spirit as we set sail for Rhegium, our first port of call, on the tip toe of Italia.[2] From there we sailed to Syracuse on the southeastern side of Sicilia[3] before making the one-hundred-mile voyage to Fair Havens. It was a long journey through the Mediterranean Sea, but at last we neared the most magnificent city on the sea!

"Look," I exclaimed, amazed at the tower that rose majestically above the sandy seaside.

"That," Pontius said, "is Strato's Tower. And the city is Caesarea."

"Ah, what a tribute to Grandfather!" I said as our ship made its way into the remarkable harbor Herod had built.

"Yes indeed," Pontius explained. "Old Herod the Great really was great all right—a great builder and a great politician. He built a magnificent city for Augustus as well, just a day's march from Jerusalem. He named that city Sebaste.[4] But, my dear Claudia," he looked down into my eyes, "it is Caesarea that will be our home while we are here in Judea. The palace shall be yours. That is only fitting. I am honored to share it with you in this great city that is named after your own illustrious grandfather."

I was filled with joy at the sweet words and sentiment of my husband. Our trip had been long and so very tiring, and now we had arrived "home"—home in Caesarea in Judea.

We had barely settled into the palace in Caesarea, when Pontius made plans to visit Jerusalem, the center of the religious and political life of this forsaken land.

"I must waste no time in setting up the Praetorium,"[5] he told me. "As governor, I will hang my shield at the gate and post my tribune on guard. I can do this anywhere," he boasted. "Right here in Caesarea if I choose, or in Jerusalem, or at Herod's Palace, or at the Antonia Fortress. Wherever I choose, that will be the judicial seat." His smile broadened at the thought of his new power.

"Where will you set it up, Pontius?"

"The most advantageous place of all—the Antonia Fortress! Its history," he said, "and its strategic location cannot be equaled! A

Hasmonean fort once stood just west of the temple area. I hear that it was originally built to protect the temple from assault. That fort is where that sly old fox, Herod, built the Antonia Fortress." My husband laughed a mirthless laugh as he continued. "He really had a triple purpose in mind," Pontius said. "It was perfect for suppressing riots, preserving order within the temple courtyards, and securing the external defense of the city at its most vulnerable point." Pontius chuckled again as he said, "And the Jews were led to believe that Herod's intent was that of protecting the temple! The fools!"

"But, Pontius, was it not strange that he named it 'The Antonia Fortress?'"

"I told you that Herod was a fox," he explained. "The very fact that he named it after Mark Antony[6] shows his true purpose—the Antonia was built with just one purpose in mind, to control Jerusalem and all of Jewish life. I heard that Josephus said, 'The city was dominated by the temple, and the temple was dominated by the Antonia.'"

Pontius was truly excited as he described the fortress. "Can you picture a gigantic quadrilateral? What a genius that Herod is! The fortress is cut almost entirely out of a rocky hill. It is mammoth, covering an area more than 450 feet one way, and 240 feet the other. Picture this, Claudia," he added. "It is protected by powerful corner towers and has numerous enclosed installations. Why those towers and installations are as grand as the palace itself!

"Not only that," he continued, "there is the most marvelous courtyard you can imagine. Huge! It is more than 7,500 feet square. This will be the place of meeting between Jerusalem and the Antonia.

"Nothing was left to chance when Antonia was built, even down to the deep water-cisterns beneath its polished pavement. Ah, the polished pavement!—a thing a beauty—and the whole courtyard is surrounded by tall cloisters," he added with a wave of his arm. "This magnificent courtyard is the heart of the fortress. This," he said proudly, "is to be my Praetorium, with its pavement par excellence!"

I was so grateful to have Julia with me in this far-away strange land. She had been my slave for as long as I could remember, and I felt that there was nothing she would not do for me. It didn't take us long to settle into the palace overlooking the beautiful Mediterranean Sea.

"I want to learn as much as I can about these people," I told her as we watched the natives on the seashore.

"I know one thing already," Julia said. "This is a proud race of people—strong willed, I hear."

"That's true," I agreed. "Pontius told me that they have their own God."

"That's not so unusual, Princess," Julia reminded me.

"I know," I told her, "but the Jews are the one people group that does not recognize or worship any other god."

"By the fortune of Caesar," Julia exclaimed. "I never heard of such a thing! Haven't these people ever heard of Jupiter, the ruler of heaven, earth, and all people and even other gods?"

"Oh," I said, "I think they have heard of him and of Mercury and Diana and all the others as well. They just won't worship them."

Julia left the room shaking her head. "By the fortune of Caesar. This is a strange people."

The next day Pontius left with his legions for Jerusalem. I had an uneasy feeling as I watched them march east, carrying their standards bearing images of my father. If these people were so determined not to recognize any other gods than their own Yahweh, how would they react to images of my father, Tiberias, who was freely worshiped by all the Roman Empire?

I spent anxious hours awaiting my husband's return. He came home to Caesarea, feeling quite confident about the whole affair, but I was plagued with clouds of apprehension.

"If those stubborn Jews attack the Antonia," he told me, "I'll see that they are severely punished for their revolt!"

"What happened?"

"It is time these stiff-necked people learn who is in command here!"

"Yes, Pontius," I said, fear clutching my heart. "But what happened? What did you do?"

He puffed up with pride. "When we reached the Roman fortress in Jerusalem, I ordered the images of your illustrious father to be put up on the walls that faced the Jewish temple."

"What?" I cried in horror. "They will be outraged! Grandfather Augustus promised them that they had immunity from worship of any god other than Yahweh. Don't you remember the great influence Herod the Great had on Grandfather because of all the political and military support he gave during all the conflicts? Pontius, Grandfather promised!"

His face turned ashen as he stormed from the room and my protests. I spent a restless night. Sleep would not come.

Early the next morning I heard muted swishing sounds. What is that? I wondered. At first I thought it was rough seas, but the sound grew louder. Then it became a roar. I peered to the east and saw the dust rising from the road. At last it became clear! It was people! A gigantic sea of humanity as far as the eye could see! I froze in terror as I saw them drawing ever nearer to the procuratorial residence. Thousands upon thousands of people!

Where did they all come from? What did they want?

The fear of impending tragedy welled up in my soul and caught in my throat as I watched them encircle the palace. I feared for all of us, but mostly for Pontius. I watched in abject fear as he made his way to the portico. He was determined to speak to them. I was astonished that he returned in but a few moments.

"What happened?" I asked. "What do they want?"

Pontius wrung his hands in despair. "I don't know," he murmured between clenched teeth. "The fools won't leave. And, by the fortune of Caesar, they are out there praying—for my soul! They will not leave! They have completely encircled the palace. They are praying!"

Moments later Julia told me about the legend of Jericho. "The ancestors of these people circled that ancient city," she told me. "They did that day after day for seven consecutive days! And then, on the seventh day, when their priests blew the trumpets, something very strange happened."

"What? What happened?" I demanded.

Julia's eyes widened as she whispered. "The people all shouted in a loud voice and when they did," Julia seemed to choke on the words as she whispered, "the city walls . . . came . . . tumbling . . . down."

"No!" I cried, envisioning the catastrophic scene.

I ran to Pontius. He was transfixed with the scene below. "Oh Pontius," I said, clutching the sleeve of his toga, "Julia has just told me the most incredible story." I watched the color drain from his face as I related the legend. He didn't speak for a moment, but stared at his clutched fists.

At last Pontius turned to his aide who stood attentively at the governor's side. The quiver in his voice was barely perceptible as he spoke. "Pollus, go at once to those, those rabble rousers. Have them select representatives to meet with me in the Agora.[7] We must deal quickly with those praying predators." I shuddered at the vehemence of Pontius' utterance, for the words oozed as poisonous venom from between his clenched teeth. "I'll speak to them there," he said, unable to mask his growing hatred for the Jews.

Orders were given for the troops to surround the Agora. They were prepared to kill any and all of the revolters at the signal that Pontius was poised to give. I watched the scene from the portico. All seven thousand rebels knelt in the square. A strange hush fell like a mantle on a sleeping giant. How eerie—thousands upon thousands of people—and not a sound! It was as though the whole world was waiting for the prearranged signal.

Pontius looked statuesque as he observed the extraordinary scene. The breeze from the Mediterranean stirred the hem of his robe, cascading small ripples of gold and white. Its restless motion was the only apparent movement in the entire Agora. The dust settled about the kneeling forms of the men, young and old. I shall never forget that sight, nor the emotion. The whole world waited for Pontius Pilate's signal to annihilate the kneeling, praying multitude.

The signal never came. Pontius turned from the platform and disappeared into the sea of troops. He came home—humiliated. He simply shook his head and murmured, "These fools would rather die than have images overlook their precious temple." Precious had become a word of vilification in Pontius' mouth.

We never spoke of the incident, but I could see the subtle change in him. He had blundered with this proud people, but he could never respond to them in kindness. I think he would have liked to have had revenge. He never met the demands of the Jews until their protests threatened to end in violence.

"I can't have this reported back to Rome," was the only thing he ever told me about the growing number of disturbing incidents.

In the meantime, I was keen to learn all that I could about the Jews. I was fascinated by their single-mindedness, by the strength of their faith, and by the courage of their convictions.

"Not all the religious ones are in the temple," Julia told me. "There is one I have heard of who baptizes in the Jordan River. His name is John, and they call him the Baptizer."

"How do you learn all these things, Julia?"

"I have come to know some of the Jewish women who work here in the palace," she explained. "Some have even become my friends. It has become easy and natural to share stories of our lives with each other."

"Julia!" I said, as an idea crossed my mind. "Do you think they would be willing to talk with me? I so want to learn their culture, their customs, their religion."

Julia's forehead furrowed into tiny crevices. "I don't know, Highness. They might be fearful to be so open with you, you being the governor's wife." Of course Julia was right. But I asked her to see, discretely, what she could learn.

One day, about a week later, Julia entered my chamber, accompanied by a young olive-skinned girl.

"Your Majesty," Julia said, bowing low. "With your permission, I'd like to introduce someone."

"Of course, Julia. I'd be delighted to meet your friend." I felt a smile cross my face as I looked at the shy girl standing beside Julia.

"This is Dorcus. She is one of our Jewish cooks."

Dorcus bowed.

"I'm happy to meet you, Dorcus."

"Thank you, Highness."

That was the beginning of my education about this proud people with a noble and long heritage.

It is interesting to note that our arrival in Judea coincided with the emergence of a Galilean rabbi, Jesus of Nazareth.

"What is a rabbi?" I asked Dorcus.

"He's a teacher, a teacher of the Law of Yahweh."

"But I thought that was the Pharisees' position."

"Well, yes," Dorcus explained, "Pharisees are teachers."

"What do they teach?" I wanted to know.

"They teach the Law—the written Law and also the oral Law," Dorcus explained. "I like that they teach about angels, who are good, and loving and kind. But, there are also demons, who are just the opposite. They don't want to help you; they want to destroy you! The Pharisees also teach that the Scriptures say that Messiah is coming."

"What is Messiah?" I asked.

A cloud of concern swept over Dorcus' youthful face. "I can't talk about that," she said hastily. "Please, Highness, may I go now?"

"Of course you may," I said, although I was disappointed.

I must talk with Julia, I decided. Perhaps she can shed light on this puzzle.

"Oh yes," Julia told me when I questioned her, "I know a little about Messiah. The Jews believe that Messiah will be a savior, and that he will come to free his people, just as Moses did when he led the Jews out of Egypt."

"Julia," I asked, "could that be why Dorcus did not want to tell me about Messiah? Do these people think we Romans are like the Egyptians—that we are keeping them in bondage? No," I said, answering my own question. "We give these people freedom. Rome has created Pax Romana, a peace that the world has never known before. Julia, you know there is no conflict; therefore, there is peace."

While I was keen to learn about the Jews, Pontius was certain he had them all figured out.

"I have a wonderful idea," he beamed one day. "We will build an aqueduct to provide fresh water for Jerusalem." He paced in happy anticipation as he went on. "There are some ancient reservoirs in Bethlehem, just six miles north of Jerusalem. That supply of fresh water will ingratiate this people to me! No more of this hatred and strife!"

"That's wonderful!" I said. "There is no doubt that we have the finest engineers and workers for the job. They cannot be surpassed. But Pontius, do we have the funds? Where will you get the money?"

"I have given this idea a great deal of thought," Pontius replied. "Just think about it, Claudia—with this project we will provide badly needed fresh water for these people. It seems only right that they provide the funds. We will use the temple treasury. It is so simple—each Jew, man and boy, will pay his share through the temple tax. We provide the blessing; they provide the funds."

Again I was uneasy about my husband's decision, but I said nothing. I had seen his temper flare with more frequency of late and decided to keep my opinion to myself, at least for the time being. I realized too late that I should have said something to him. The plans were made and set in motion. The aqueduct was built. But not with the result Pontius had expected.

"Get the troops ready!" he demanded of his aides. "There's a riot in Jerusalem. Will this people never understand? Why, oh why don't they appreciate all that I do for them?"

"Or to them," I heard some nameless, faceless man mutter.

In obedience, the troops set off for Jerusalem, but not in the traditional military fashion. I saw them leave in plain clothes. Why were they not in uniform? I wondered. What mad scheme is this? What evil will come from this action?

"Oh, such shame, Highness," Julia told me later, relating events she had heard from one of the soldiers. "Such horror ensued!" Sobs shook her troubled being. "Oh, Highness," she cried, "they suppressed the riot all right!" The tears ran down her cheeks as she grieved for her many new friends, fearing the worse. "But Highness, in the doing, in the suppression, thousands of people panicked and were trodden to death!"

A pall hung over the palace for weeks. It didn't get any better when we heard from Rome. Father and the Senate were very angry with my husband for the bad judgment he had shown in this "incident."

"Claudia," Pontius said in one of our rare moments together, "this reprimand from Rome seriously undermines my authority. I suspect that information reached your father by way of the high priest's intelligence service."[8] He was so distraught that I thought he would cry. Instead he hurled his cup at the far wall and stormed out of the room.

While Pilate ruled Judea, I continued to learn more about the Jewish people.

Dorcus told me about a strange group of people—the Essenes. "They withdrew from the rest of Jewish society," she explained. "They wanted to be a pure nation, separate from the Hellenized Jews.[9] The Essenes believe these people have lost their perspective of Yahweh."

"I've heard of Sadducees," I said. "What can you tell me about them, Dorcus?"

"They represent the vested interests of the Jews in Jerusalem. They have the best standing with Rome, but they are terribly unpopular with the Jewish people."

"Why?"

"Because," Dorcus explained, "they keep aloof from us. We are too common for them. The Sadducees include nobles and high priests who dominate the temple and all its ritual."

I must warn Pontius about them, I thought. They sound dangerous.

There were others too. Dorcus told me about the Zealots. They frightened me too. From what I could tell, they were the hotheads, ready for insurrection.

"Most people do not talk much about the Herodians," Dorcus explained. "But they support the Herod family—they were the ones who wanted Herod on the throne. Actually, of all the Jewish group, the Herodians are the truest friends of Rome. They not only want to maintain the Herodian dynasty, but they are very interested in keeping the Pax Romana."

This was a lot for me to digest, but Dorcus said there was more. "There's another group," she said, "a new group. It is gaining popularity, or ill will, depending on your point of view. It is led by Jesus, the rabbi from Nazareth."

"I've heard about Jesus," I said. "Tell me more about him. What is he like?"

Dorcus face brightened. "I saw him once," she said. "He came to Jerusalem for the Passover. Oh, the crowds that follow that beloved rabbi!" She radiated her delight in having seen the Master, as she called him.

"He had just come from Cana, from a wedding," she said. "While he was there, he turned water into wine. Imagine that! The wine steward was in a panic. But Jesus had water brought to him, the water in the jars for purification no less. And with just a word from the Master, the water was no longer water! It was wine! What a miracle!"

Dorcus told me more as her confidence and trust in me grew. She told me of other things Jesus had done, miraculous things. Can you imagine: he walked on water! She said that Jesus had fed thousands of people with a few fish and loaves, and that he had cured people's diseases. He had even raised people from the dead!

His teaching, too, was unique. "He teaches as one with authority," Dorcus told me as she related some of the wisdom and beauty of his words.

I once caught a brief glimpse of him myself, and I must admit that my heart skipped a beat as our eyes met. What eyes! They could look into your very soul. I felt that I could never keep a secret from him. He would just know.

Pontius and I had settled into life at Caesarea, but I seldom noticed its beauty any longer. My concern for my husband was growing deeper with every passing day. To be sure Pontius was fulfilling his responsibilities. But he had no compassion for the people he had been sent to govern. He never really came to know their heart and soul. I grieve that he had not given me more opportunity to tell him all that I had learned from Dorcus. But he was single-minded, stubborn, some might say. Still, because of his many blunders, he had suffered a great deal of humiliation at the hands of these people. As a result, he had become vulnerable, and I fear, less capable of ruling. And all of this led to the tragic events of that Passover season three years after our arrival in Israel.

I used to wonder about Passover. The first time I heard the word I wondered—what, or who, passed over what or whom? It was Julia who explained the significance of that event in Egypt so many centuries ago—how the captive people were set free from slavery. She explained that the sign of the lambs' blood on the doorposts was the signal for the Angel of Death to "pass over" their houses and not take the firstborn children of their families.

"Every year the Israelites, the Children of Israel, as they like to call themselves, celebrate this most sacred event in their national and religious history," Julia explained. "Jesus is no exception."

"It is baffling, Julia," I said. "Why would he risk coming?" I shook my head in disbelief as I said, "I have heard all the controversy surrounding him. Not everyone is pleased with his outspoken debates with the hierarchy of his outrageous religion."

At great personal risk, three years after he had begun his ministry and we had come from Rome, Jesus came again to Jerusalem to celebrate Passover.

"In the three years that we have been here," Pontius complained, "I have never known Jerusalem to be so crowded with rabble. Passover!" He spit out the word as though it were a curse. "Why can't these people be civilized like the Romans and celebrate without their sacrifices and orgies!"

"But, Pontius," I said, seeing a tantrum coming on, "we sacrifice to our gods!"

"Yes, but we do it with dignity. We don't all go in great swells of humanity clamoring to the priest to kill our offerings! Oh, by the fortune of Caesar, Claudia, I shall never understand these people!"

It was too late to reason with him; his tantrum had begun. This time he flung his javelin across the room, barely missing the porter who stood nearby. "We have done so much for them, and what thanks do we get? What?" There was no way to respond, for he continued his tirade, eyes blazing, muscles tensed. "Insurrection! Rebellion! Why, just today we arrested another Jew, Barabbas! Like so many others, this Zealot is bent on bringing down our government and destroying the Pax Romana we have so carefully established in this citadel of stupidity and crime!"

Pontius turned on his heel to leave the room. He turned at the doorway. "I'm off to Jerusalem now. Perhaps my presence will quiet things there!" He turned then, and in a clatter of agitation, was gone.

"How can Pontius' presence in Jerusalem quiet things?" I wondered. "It never has before!"

An eerie spirit of gloom fell upon the palace. The activities that seemed so familiar and routine yesterday took on a dream-like quality today. Although it was a warm spring day, there was a chill of doom overshadowing the palace, like a black mantle flung over a decaying corpse. Fear and anxiety overwhelmed me. My spirit was depleted. I was bone weary by day's end.

"Julia," I said after my evening bath, "I can't stay up another moment. I'm going to bed."

I tossed and turned and finally fell into a fretful sleep. Visions of disaster invaded my slumber. Horror filled my soul in my nightmare state. Demons, flashing lightning in horrible sequences flooded the eyes of my imagination. And in the center of all this fearful apprehension was the face of—of whom? I tried desperately to make out his features. It was like looking at someone through a heavy veil. At last, in a great downward motion, the veil was torn in two. The face became clear. In a moment of fearful clarity I saw who it was. "No!" my anxious heart cried. But, yes, it was Jesus! Jesus of Nazareth. I awoke with a start, sitting bolt upright on my bed.

"Julia! Julia!" I called out in terror. The poor dear came flying into my chamber on winged feet to attend my summons.

"Julia," I said, scribbling a note, "take this to one of the palace guards. Have him take it to Governor Pilate. At once!" She was off again, her sandaled feet barely touching the floor as she went to fulfill her mission.

I reread the note in my mind, imagining Pontius' response to my plea: "Pontius. Please! Do not have anything to do with Jesus for I have suffered many things today in a dreadful dream because of him."[10]

I prayed to my gods. I even prayed to the Israelite God, Yahweh! "Oh please. Be merciful to Jesus of Nazareth. Let nothing evil befall him! I sense he is a holy man."

Sleep would not come after that. I paced the marble floor as I awaited word. I watched for the return of the troops from Jerusalem. Peering east into the predawn gloom, I pondered all the events of the past three years. Pontius had turned from a promising young diplomat into a blustering bully—or worse. Tears of helplessness coursed their weary way down my sallow cheeks. No point pondering, I sighed, turning from the window to face another bleak day.

Time dragged on, and by late morning the stillness had become an overwhelming blanket of doom. Unknown demons plagued my thoughts. Even the servants were subdued. All was hushed, and waiting. Then, at about the sixth hour, an ominous darkness clouded everything. The gloom seeped into my very soul. Try as I might, thoughts of hopelessness lurked in the deep recesses of my mind.

Julia quietly entered my chamber to announce that the midday meal had been prepared. "Won't you come, Highness?" she pleaded. "You have had nothing to eat all day."

"No, Julia, not now," I said, adding, "maybe later." She left me to my reverie.

I do not know how long this lethargy clung to me, but at about the ninth hour a new terror assaulted my senses. I had just resumed my position at the east window, peering into the blackness, when I felt a rippling movement beneath my feet. "What?" I started. "Could it be an earthquake? There! There it is again!" The second jolt seemed a bit more severe. It sent my blue porcelain vase crashing to the floor. I felt the floor sway beneath my feet. "By all the gods," I thought, "we shall all die!"

But as quickly as the tremors had begun, they subsided, and then ceased. Julia ran into the room and we grasped the comfort of each other's arms, embracing against the dread of the unknown.

"Highness," Julia said at last, stepping away. "Please, forgive my presumption."

"There is nothing to forgive," I assured her. "We are two friends consoling one another against the terrors of the day."

At last the dreadful day came to an end with my husband's return from Jerusalem. The sun had reappeared, but the pall remained.

"What happened, Pontius?" I demanded, hoping that he had heeded my warning about my dream of Jesus.

"I did what I could," he said, averting his eyes from mine. I knew then that the outcome was not what I had hoped.

"What happened?" I repeated.

"Those fools!" His hostility echoed against the walls of the great room. "The Sanhedrin[11] held a trial!" The mockery in his voice cut through the air like a sword. He began pacing as he related the events of this long, salient day. "Of course they arrested him! Jesus has become much too well known, and," he added with fervor, "popular! He was bound and led from a garden to a hearing before Annas. When he was through with Jesus, the old man sent him to his son-in-law, Caiaphas.[12] Caiaphas wanted Jesus to die. I know! I heard what he said just a week ago, 'It is expedient that one man should die for the people.' Claudia! He was talking about Jesus!"

Why? I wondered silently as Pontius continued to relate the horrible events.

"Well, Claudia," he said, "they brought the wretch to me for judgment. The sons of folly would not enter the Praetorium! They said that they did not want to defile themselves before Passover!" Pontius' anger almost overwhelmed him as he recalled the insult. "No, they would not enter, but Jesus did.

"I asked, 'What is the charge?' As usual they played word games with me, saying 'We would not have turned him over to you if he were not a criminal.' I told them to take Jesus and judge him by their own laws. You know, Claudia, I do believe these people have too much freedom. Ah, but there we were, at odds over the law. They reminded me that only Romans have the authority to execute someone.

"I had Jesus brought before me. I questioned him myself. 'Are You the King of the Jews?' He answered my question with one of his own. He had the audacity to say, 'Is this your own question, or did others tell you about me?'

"What insolence! So, I said, 'Am I a Jew? Your own people brought you here. Tell me, Jesus, what have you done?' Then he told me that his Kingdom is not of this world. Claudia, what other world is there? He told me that he was born to be a King, and that everyone who is of the truth recognizes him.

"'What is truth?' I asked him. I didn't wait for his answer, but turned to go to the portico to talk again to the Jews. I personally announced that I found no fault in Jesus. Then I gave them a choice. I would release one man in honor of their holy season, Passover. 'I will release to you, the King of the Jews.' Can you

believe these people, can you? Jesus, a man who had such a following, now out of favor with his own people.

"Claudia, I can still hear them shouting, 'No, not Jesus! Release
Barabbas! Crucify Jesus! Crucify Him!'"

I felt faint at these words. "No, Pontius, no, not that!"

"Yes, Claudia," he said, head lowered. "I had no options. I had a
basin brought to me, and I symbolically washed my hands of Jesus'
blood."

Pontius was forever haunted by that act of submission to the mob.

Jesus had come to Jerusalem to celebrate the Passover with his disciples. "He made significant changes in the sacred meal," Dorcus
told me. "I overheard that he said that he himself was the sacrifice—
that it was his blood that would create the difference between life and
death for believers. Jesus said that people would no longer have to
fear death, for he had conquered it."

"Is that what Messiah means?" I asked.

"Yes," she answered softly, "Messiah means Anointed One, Savior. And Jesus is the Messiah, the Savior, not only of the Jews, but as
he said, for all who would accept him. He said he came to serve, not
to be served."

"How strange for one called King of the Jews," I thought as Dorcus continued.

"Jesus even washed the feet of his disciples at the Passover meal—
he even washed the feet of that betrayer Judas! That was Jesus' example that his followers are to serve one another."

It was Julia who added, "Princess Claudia, you must have heard
about Judas! Everyone in all of Judea has."

"No," I admitted.

"Judas," Julia said, "friend turned traitor. What irony!"

I did not know at the time that Jesus had to die. I did not know
that he had been born to die. I did not understand the sacrifice he had
to make, nor the sacrifice he had to be.

All that took place in Pontius' third year of his appointment as
Governor. He had seven more bitter years yet to serve in Judea. His
frustration increased over the years, as did his lack of mercy. As his
cruelty grew worse, we grew further apart.

He was humiliated on several occasions. Ultimately he had to back
down from another excessive decree. For years golden shields of por-
traits of Father and other Roman notables adorned the walls of

Herod's citadel. He had to acquiesce to a demand of the Pharisees to remove them.

Shortly after that, predictably, he made his final and fatal mistake. A crowd of Samaritans gathered for a religious ceremony on Mount Gerizim.[13] Unthinking, Pontius interpreted their religious unrest as an act of revolt and brutally—yes, brutally—wiped out an entire neighboring village in reprisal. That terrible act was reported to Vitellius.[14] As a result, Pontius was summoned to Antioch to be tried. His trial didn't last long. The verdict—guilty! Pontius Pilate was ordered back to Rome.

Terrible things happen to people. And people do terrible things. But my eyes had met the eyes of One to whom terrible things had been done, but who had never done anything but good. I heard that he was buried in a cave near Golgatha after the crucifixion.

Jesus died. Yes, he did.
Jesus was buried. Yes, he was.
But that same Jesus rose, he rose from the dead. Yes, he did.
He is alive today! He lives eternally!
And wonder of wonders, I, too, can have eternal life. Yes, I can. How?
By acknowledging these very facts:
He died.
He was buried.
He rose from the dead.
Jesus died for me, and he lives for me.
And as I die to self and live for Jesus—I can have eternal life!
Yes, and so can you.

NOTES

1. Although Scripture does not record her name, many scholars believe Claudia Procula was Pilate's wife.

2. Italia was the old name for modern Italy.

3. Sicilia was the old name for modern Sicily.

4. Sebaste was the Greek name for Augustus.

5. The Praetorium was the judicial seat of a Roman governor.

6. Mark Antony was the Roman conqueror of Syria and Palestine.

7. Agora was a Roman market place.

8. There was an intricate intelligence network throughout the Roman Empire, among which was that under the authority of Israel's high priest, who regularly sent intelligence information to the authorities in Rome.

9. Hellenized Jews were Greek-speaking Jews of the Dispersion who had adopted Greek habits and customs.

10. Matthew 27:19, paraphrased.

11. The Jewish ruling body was called the Sanhedrin. The following account of Jesus' trial is based primarily on the Gospel of John. Only Matthew's Gospel records the incident where Pilate washes his hands of Jesus' blood (see Matthew 27:24).

12. Caiaphas was the high priest during Jesus' adult ministry.

13. Mount Gerizim was the traditional place of worship for the Samaritan people.

14. Vitellius was the Roman legate of Syria, to whom Pilate was accountable.

Salome, Mary Magdalene, Joanna

They Walked with Jesus

THE SKIES CRY AND THE FISH DON'T BITE

Going on from there, He [Jesus] saw two other brothers, James the son of Zebedee, and John his brother, in the boat with Zebedee their father, mending their nets. He called them, and immediately they left the boat and their father, and followed Him.[1]

It's raining today. My husband, Zebedee, won't like that. He says the fish seem to hide when it rains. Our sons, James and John, storm and thunder just like their father when the weather is like this.

I can hear Zebedee now—bellowing his displeasure, "Salome, this fishing business will be the death of me yet!"

But Zebedee bellowed about something else recently, loud and clear. He thundered his indignation that our sons "up and left the business!" I couldn't believe my ears, but that's what he said. James and John were on the boat, mending the nets, when along came this carpenter from Nazareth.

"'Follow me,' was all he said," my husband told me. "And, Salome," he added, incredulous, "they did!"

This story takes approximately forty-five minutes to present orally.
For more ideas, see "Hints for Presenters" at the beginning of this book.

"But," I argued, "our sons are disciples of John the Baptizer! Following an itinerant preacher from southern Galilee is not my idea of a career for them!"

Our fishing business was good. We had some very important clients, like Caiaphas, the high priest. Our son John can see him almost any time he wishes. And with influential people like that buying our fish, well, there's no doubt that our success is secure.

"What's a mother to do?" I wondered, upset and confused—that is, until I met Jesus myself.

I was busy directing the evening meal when I heard them enter the courtyard. I turned. There were my sons, James and John. A stranger was with them. "Could this be Jesus?" I wondered. Why, he's no taller nor distinguished looking than any other thirty-year-old man in Judea.

But there was something in his manner that set him apart. He was poised, yet he possessed an air of humility. He didn't wait for my greeting of welcome, but wished me "Shalom."

"This is Rabbi Jesus bar Joseph," James said.

"Yes," John echoed. "He has wanted to meet you."

"Shalom, Rabbi," I greeted. "Will you honor us as our guest at dinner?" (Not to be hospitable would be a serious breach of etiquette, one I was not willing to commit.)

"Yes," he responded warmly, adding, "it is I who am honored."

By then Zebedee had joined us. When he learned that the rabbi would be our guest, he ordered a servant to fetch a basin and towel to wash Jesus' feet.

Jesus' presence gave the evening a feeling of surrealism. It was clear that he possessed great spiritual depth. When he spoke, it was with confident authority. Not vindictively, you understand, but with reflection and compassion. He made the Scriptures come alive.

The words he articulated from David's songbook still echo in my heart, "I will sing of the mercies of the Lord forever; with my mouth will I make known your faithfulness to all generations. For I have said, 'Mercy shall be built up forever; your faithfulness you shall establish in the very heavens.' I have made a covenant with my chosen, I have sworn to my servant David, 'Your seed I will establish forever, and build up your throne to all generations.'"[2]

Jesus' rendering of this, one of my favorite passages of Scripture, filled my soul with joyful anticipation. I understood then why my sons had become disciples of Jesus of Nazareth, for I was ready to join their ranks.

ENCOUNTER AT AN OASIS

The Lord is my strength and my song, and He has become my salvation.[3]

Life is not easy, especially when one is identified with a sinful city, or worse yet, a sinful past. I know all the stories that have been told about me. I don't know how they got started, but somehow they did. Maybe it's because I'm from Magdala.

Have you heard of that city on the west shore of the Sea of Galilee? When folks learned that I came from that city, they began to call me Mary Magdalene. That wouldn't have been so bad, but the city had a reputation for being a haven for prostitutes. Maybe that's why people thought that my seven demons were a direct correlation to a life of sin and degradation.

They were right about my having seven demons though. Those demons plagued me for as long as I could remember. They made my life a nightmare. I avoided everyone—that is, until Jesus.

"He's been preaching and healing in every village along the coast of the Sea of Galilee!" That's what people were saying all over Magdala.

It's hard to have faith when one has been afflicted all one's life. I had become embittered about God, yet resigned to my condition, I thought. Now, with those words about Jesus, a glimmer of hope was kindled within my soul.

"Is it possible?" I wondered. "No, how can that be?" I reasoned. Yet, dim hope is better than no hope at all.

It took all the strength I possessed to follow the crowd that pursued the healer from Nazareth. It seemed as though my seven demons had multiplied to keep me from my quest. But my desire for healing strengthened me in the fray against the evil that had overtaken my life. I kept going. The other seekers were soon beyond my field of vision because I could no longer keep pace with their long strides toward our common goal.

"I will not be deterred!" my weary heart vowed. And finally, my perseverance was rewarded. I knew the healer was close at hand. The overwhelming crowd looming ahead indicated his presence in their midst. With renewed vigor, I continued my pilgrimage. I was determined to get as close to the rabbi as I could. I was prepared to push and shove my way through if I had to. But when I reached the edge of the crowd I was amazed at how freely I was able to make my way through the assembled mass of people. It was as though a path had been opened for me, and before I knew it—I stood before him—Jesus, the healer.

He was seated on a rock, arms outstretched. "Come to me, all you who labor and are heavy laden, and I will give you rest." His eyes met mine as he said, "Take my yoke upon you and learn from me, for I am gentle and lowly in heart, and you will find rest for your souls. For my yoke is easy and my burden is light."[4]

Tears of hope filled my eyes as I fell to my knees before him. "Oh, Jesus," I whispered, "I need rest. I need healing."

"My daughter," he said as he gently placed his hands upon my bowed head. "Your faith has made you well." The demons were gone, replaced with sweet shalom.

FROM THE COURTS OF HEROD TO THE PLAINS OF GALILEE

Blessed is the man who walks not in the counsel of the ungodly, nor stands in the path of sinners, nor sits in the seat of the scornful . . . [5]

My husband, Chuza, had very little time for me. Even though we had an active social life, I was often lonely.

"Joanna," he would say, "you know that as administrator in Herod Antipas' court, I am expected to entertain certain people. And, as my wife, you must be with me in this." Of course he was right, and yet . . .

We lived in Herod's Tiberias palace in Galilee, so it was not surprising to hear rumors. Among the most intriguing were those regarding a traveling preacher from Nazareth in the hill country to the southeast. My curiosity piqued when I heard that he even healed a woman from Magdala who had seven demons. "Well," I thought, "the only demon plaguing me is boredom."

But that boredom was enough to motivate me to action. I joined the pilgrims who went to see this man for themselves. The crowd soon grew to overwhelming proportions, a virtual sea of humanity. We trudged on like a giant dragon wending its way in a tedious journey, relentless in pursuit of its prey. And then, I saw him, seated on a grassy knoll, a little apart from the throng. There was a smaller group pressing close to him. I counted them; there were twelve. Their eyes were riveted upon Jesus' face. Beyond them was the multitude. I became one of their number.

He was speaking. His words were exquisite gems of wisdom and exhortation. "Blessed are the poor in spirit,"[6] he began.

Poor? In spirit? I pondered. My interest heightened as he continued. Each blessing he rendered was rich with spiritual significance as well as instruction for a life lived to the fullest. No longer feeling plagued by boredom, I had never felt more alive!

"I must meet him!" I concluded. I waited beside a sycamore tree as the crowds began to disperse. The sun was already setting as I made my way through the remaining disciples, but I was determined to speak with Jesus. I raised my eyes as I neared my goal. His gentle gaze was fixed on me. It was as though he already knew my mission and my thoughts.

"Master," I managed.

"Yes, daughter," he said, reaching his hand toward mine.

"I am Joanna," I said, "wife of Chuza, the steward in Herod's house."

"Yes," was his only response.

Did he already know? I wondered.

"I see you have women in your company," I said. "And if you will, I would join them." I thrust my moneybag into his hand. "I am a woman of some wealth," I said. "I would like to help in the support of your work."

He thanked me and smiled as he handed the bag to one of his disciples. I became one of his company from that moment on. Boredom was lifted, replaced by an overwhelming assurance of grace and a passion for the ministry and teaching of this man.

SALOME: HER BOUNTY AND HER HEART

If anyone desires to come after me, let him deny himself, and take up his cross, and follow me.[7]

After dinner, Jesus left. Zebedee and I, along with our sons, James and John, retired to the courtyard.

"Come, Salome," my husband insisted. "Let us sit in the coolness of the night. It's been a long day."

We took our favorite seats beneath the spreading branches of the fig tree. "Zebedee," I said, "I can see now why our sons have been drawn to Jesus."

"He certainly knows Scripture," my husband responded.

"Oh, it's more than that," James added. "He lives it."

"Yes," John agreed, excitement brightening his youthful face as he recited a familiar benediction followed by the stirring Shema. "Blessed be the Lord our God for the glory of his handiwork and for the light-giving lights which he has made for his praise. Selah! Blessed be the Lord our God, who has formed the lights.[8] Hear, O Israel: The Lord our God, the Lord is one! You shall love the Lord your God with all your heart, with all your soul, and with all your might. And these words which I command you today shall be in your heart."[9]

John concluded, "Jesus makes those words come alive, for the love of the Lord is displayed not only in his heart and soul, but with all his strength and might."

"Could he be the Messiah?" Zebedee reflected solemnly.

"Oh yes!" James insisted. "When Jesus was baptized, an amazing thing happened!"

"Immediately after the baptism," John explained, "as soon as Jesus came up out of the water, the heavens were opened to him and he saw the Spirit of God coming down in the form of a dove. And then! A voice from heaven said 'This is my beloved Son in whom I am wonderfully pleased.'"[10]

I was convinced. I made a silent pledge that, from that day forward, I would do all in my power to support Rabbi Jesus bar Joseph out of the bounty of my possessions and the toil of my hands. He already had my heart.

MARY, FREE AT LAST!

I will sing to the Lord, because he has dealt bountifully with me.[11]

I soon learned that there were other women among Jesus' disciples. Salome spent as much time as she could in our company, but often had to return home to see to her household. Ah, but how she looked after her sons, James and John, when she was with us. She would do anything for them. And when she returned from home, she always came back with a bag of coins to help provide for the needs of Jesus and his disciples.

I was glad I had nothing to take me from my Master's presence. He gave me my life, which had been lost. No! It was more than that. He *became* my life. Just to be near him was delight. To hear him speak was joy. To have his eyes meet mine was ecstasy. I never wanted to leave him. When he said my name—*Mary*—it became a thing of beauty. I was whole when I was with him.

"Mary, Mary," he said, "most assuredly, I say to you, he who hears my word and believes in him who sent me has everlasting life, and shall not come into judgment, but has passed from death into life."[12]

"Yes, Master, I do hear your word. I do believe in Yahweh who sent you. I have passed from death, the death of seven demons, and now I live. I live because of you, Jesus! How can I thank you?"

JOANNA, A TIARA EXCHANGED FOR AN APRON

Be of good courage, and he shall strengthen your heart, all you who hope in the Lord.[13]

I had no idea what being away from the palace would be like. I had no servants here in the hills of Galilee. As a matter of fact, I had become one myself.

Salome and I were on our way to Capernaum to purchase food one cloudy afternoon. "How do you do it?" I asked.

"Do what?" she responded.

"Why, all this—marketing, grinding, cooking, preparing meals. I know you have servants back home, just as I do. I'm finding this very difficult," I complained.

Salome stopped on the path and turned to look me square in the eye. "Joanna," she said at length, "you must give yourself time. This is all new to you. Yes, I do have servants at home, but I work along-side them. So, this is easier for me than it is for you. I'm accustomed to it. You're learning."

"I know you're right," I said. "But sometimes I think I should just support Jesus with my denari and not my person. But, Salome, I need to be near him, to hear his teaching."

Just then we were joined by Mary Magdalene. "Look at Mary," Salome said. "She's learning too."

I was puzzled. What was Mary learning?

"She's learning to live without demons," Salome explained, seeing my confusion.

"And what are you learning?" Mary laughed.

"I'm learning to trust more in Jesus and less in myself," Salome said, echoing Mary's laughter.

"I guess I'm learning to be meek, as Jesus teaches," I added. "I know that I already hunger and thirst for righteousness."[14]

We continued on our way to Capernaum, three women devoted to the Master. We were so different, often coming to very different conclusions about Jesus' teaching, but never differing in our devotion to him. Jesus was the catalyst for our friendship.

SALOME—A MOTHER'S AMBITION

> Then the mother of James and John, the sons of Zebedee, brought them to Jesus and respectfully asked a favor.[15]

It was a troubling time. The entire entourage was on its way to Jerusalem. The Passover was just days away. I spent as much time as I could with my sons, James and John, as we walked along. But Jesus suddenly stopped on that dusty road.

"Come aside," he said to the twelve. The rest of us, including Mary Magdalene, Joanna, and I, stood aside as Jesus and his closest disciples made their way out of earshot.

"Storm clouds are gathering," Mary said as we looked at the knot of men surrounding our Lord. "Jesus' enemies are close at hand." I could see the worry etched at the corners of her dark eyes.

Joanna absentmindedly examined a coriander plant growing at the side of the road. She fingered its delicate leaves as she said, "My anxiety grows with every passing day. Chuza has spoken of Herod's growing interest in Jesus. I'm worried."

I added my voice of concern, "More than once the Master has said that the Son of Man would be betrayed into the hands of men, and they will kill him, but he added something very strange—that on the third day he would be raised up."[16]

Neither woman responded to my words. Each was deep in thought, as was I. Finally, Jesus and the others joined us. Our journey was about to resume. But I had something on my mind. I'd been giving it a great deal of thought in recent days—ever since Jesus had spoken about the kingdom of heaven.

As the disciples began retrieving their burdens, I took the opportunity to speak to Jesus. I bowed before the Master. "I must ask you something, Rabbi," I said.

"What is it you wish, Salome?" he said affectionately.

"Oh, Jesus," I began, "you have spoken of your kingdom on several occasions."

"Yes," he agreed.

I could feel the rhythm of my heart beating within my breast like the swift fluttering of a sparrow's wings against the angry sky.

"Jesus," I began, "could you . . . is it possible. . . ?" I cleared my dry throat and implored, "Will you permit my two sons, James and John, to sit on thrones next to yours?"

The troubled look that appeared on his face disturbed me. "Salome," he said, "you don't know what you are asking."

Then Jesus turned to James and John and asked them, "Are you able to drink from the terrible cup I am about to drink from?"

Without hesitation, they replied, "Oh yes, Master, we are able."

My blood turned cold with Jesus' next words, "You shall indeed drink from it. But it is not for me to say who will sit on the thrones next to mine. The Father will decide."

The other disciples overheard my request and the response of Jesus, as well as that of James and John. They turned on my sons with bitter words.

"Who do you think you are?" they demanded. "What makes you think that when Jesus comes into his kingdom, you will have higher authority than any of us?"

But Jesus had a lesson for us that day, one that I had trouble understanding. He said that if one wants to be a leader, one must first learn to be a servant. What? Preposterous!

I thought of my own servants and didn't comprehend until Jesus said, "Your attitude must be like mine, for I, the Messiah, did not come to be served, but to serve, and to give my life as a ransom for many."[17]

We went on then, for Jesus had set his face for Jerusalem.

JOANNA REJOICES IN JESUS' TRIUMPH

Behold, your King is coming to you; . . . lowly, and riding on a donkey, a colt, the foal of a donkey.[18]

All thoughts of doom were left on that dusty road near Bethphage on the Mount of Olives that sunny Sunday morning. The crowd was the largest I'd ever seen, everyone intent on celebrating the Passover in Jerusalem. It was clear that even though the pilgrimage to Jerusalem was always a special event, this one had aspects never before imagined.

What made it so? It was the Master who created the air of excitement and anticipation. What Jesus did was unprecedented. I still feel the thrill as I remember him riding triumphantly on a colt into Jerusalem, the City of David, the Holy City!

Everyone caught the excitement. Mary Magdalene was the first to throw the palm fronds she was carrying onto the path before Jesus. Everyone followed her animated example. I even saw people spread their cloaks on the road leading to Jerusalem—the road on which the Master's donkey trod.

I gleefully joined the chorus of voices exclaiming, "Hosanna to the Son of David! Blessed is he who comes in the name of the Lord! Hosanna in the highest!"

I've attended gala celebrations at the palace in Tiberias, even grand affairs at Herod's palace in Jerusalem. But no event, no excitement, nothing compared with the exuberant joy I experienced that beautiful Sunday when the road to Jerusalem became a carpet of palms and garments to welcome my Lord. Hosanna to my Master, the Son of David!

Then at last we arrived in the Holy City. All of Jerusalem was there, puzzled by this turn of events.

"Who is this?" they asked. All of us who had been with him throughout Galilee knew. And the pilgrims who had joined us in welcoming him knew.

"This," we responded, "is Jesus, the prophet from Nazareth![19] This is our king, come to free us from the oppressors."

Jesus dismounted the donkey and strode up the steps of the temple, disappearing in a crowd of merchants and moneychangers.

Mary Magdalene, Salome, and I exchanged anxious glances.

GLORY IN THE GARDEN—MARY AND MAJESTY

And the women who came with him from Galilee followed after, and they observed the tomb and how his body was laid. Then they returned and prepared the spices and fragrant oils. And they rested on the Sabbath according to the commandment.[20]

I cried until there were no more tears. The Master dead! was all my weary heart could feel. I had thought he was the Messiah! I would have welcomed my demons' return if it meant Jesus would still be with us.

"This is more than I can bear!" I cried aloud, beating my breast in my distress.

"A calamity beyond measure," Joanna added, her tears falling freely.

"What will happen to us now?" Salome questioned in dismay. "All the disciples have gone into hiding. The only one who stood with us at the cross was my own dear son, John, just a young man. But now he is taking on the responsibility of caring for Jesus' mother." She shook her head in disbelief and anxiety.

"It will soon be dawn," I reminded my friends. "We have one last act of service to our Master." That reminder only made the flow of tears return.

I rose from my seat. Salome and Joanna followed my lead. The spices and the fragrant oils had been prepared. Now our hearts had to be prepared for the task ahead. None of us relished the idea, and yet, it would be our last loving act for our dear Jesus.

Joanna was the first out the door of the upper room where we had been meeting with the other disciples.

"Come," she urged. "The sun will soon be up. We must get to the garden, to the tomb where they laid our Lord."

We made our way through the silent, narrow streets of Jerusalem. A dog barked as we passed through the gate at the eastern edge of the city, the same gate through which we had passed on the day before Passover, the day our Lord was crucified. The three of us stumbled along, unable to talk, barely able to see because of the predawn darkness and our tears of anguish.

I drew my cloak closer to my trembling body as we entered the garden where Jesus had been laid.

"I'm so glad," Salome said, breaking my reverie, "so glad that Jesus was laid in a tomb where no one else has lain before."

"Yes," Joanna said. "It seems fitting that he not be defiled by death, even the death of others."

"There," I said, pointing in the gloom. "Over there is the cave where they laid him." We hastened our steps and then . . .

"Where's the stone?" Joanna cried. "How could it be rolled away?"

"Oh, no!" I exclaimed. "Do you think someone has stolen our Master's body?"

The others tried to console me, but it was clear that they were as distraught as I. Even the soldiers who had been left to guard the tomb were gone. And when we looked into the tomb, we discovered that Jesus' body was gone too!

"What shall we do?" Joanna cried. "Where can we look? Who will help us?"

"Look!" Salome said, directing our attention to the two men standing beside the tomb.

They were arrayed in garments shining like the sun. I couldn't bear to look and averted my eyes toward the ground. A tremor of fear overtook me.

Then one of them spoke. "Why do you seek the living among the dead?" Before we could respond, the other man, if he was a man, said, "He is not here, but is risen! Remember how he spoke to you when he was still in Galilee, saying 'the Son of Man must be delivered into the hands of sinful men, and be crucified, and on the third day rise again.'"[21]

I remembered! A flood of hope surged through my being like a bolt of lightning. I looked up. The men were gone.

"Jesus has risen!" I said. "Hurry, we must go tell the others! He is risen from the dead, just as he said!"

Could it be? Could it really be? All that Jesus had taught us through his miracles and his words flooded our minds as we raced back to tell the others.

Peter and John ran back to the garden tomb. I tried to keep pace with them, but their long legs outpaced me. I got there just as John stooped down and looked inside, but it was Peter who went in. I waited breathlessly. Then he emerged from the tomb, his face aglow. John could wait no longer. He entered the tomb, and when he came out, he, too, had the glow of revelation on his countenance.

"I believe!" he announced. "The linen cloths are lying there," he said, "just like a cocoon, just as though Jesus arose, without even disturbing them. And there, where he was laid, is the handkerchief that encased his head. It's still in the place where it had been before Jesus left! I believe!" he repeated in rapturous joy. "Now I understand what Messiah meant when he said he would come alive again!"

He and Peter ran from the garden. They had forgotten that I was there, or perhaps they had never been aware of my presence. But I couldn't leave. And then, through my tears, I saw this man.

"Oh, sir," I beseeched him. (I thought he was the gardener.) "If you have carried him away, tell me where you have laid him, and I will take him away."

"Mary," he said softly.

Why, it was Jesus! No one says my name as does my Lord, with such love and tenderness.

"Rabboni!" I cried. "It is true! You have risen!" I wanted to cling to him, but he prevented me because he said he had not yet ascended to the Father.

"But go," he said, "tell the others that I am ascending to my Father and your Father, and to my God and your God."[22]

Jesus, my Healer, my Master, my Savior!
Salome wanted someone to fulfill her dreams for her sons.
Joanna looked for a cause.
I desired healing.
We found more than our desires, our causes, our healing. We found the Savior. You can too! Meet him now, at the empty tomb.

NOTES

1. Matthew 4:21–22. (All Scripture quoted in this chapter is from the New King James Version unless otherwise indicated.)

2. Psalm 89:1–4.

3. Psalm 118:14.

4. Matthew 11:28–30.

5. Psalm 1:1.

6. Matthew 5:3.

7. Matthew 16:24.

8. There were certain prayers that Jesus not only heard, but probably shared. This benediction may have been one of them (from Alfred Edersheim, *Sketches of Jewish Social Life in the Days of Christ*. Grand Rapids: Wm. B. Eerdmans, 1993, 269).

9. Deuteronomy 6:4–6.

10. Matthew 3:16–17, paraphrased. Also note that the Trinity is present here: The Son was baptized, the Spirit descended in the form of a dove, and the Father spoke.

11. Psalm 13:6.

12. John 5:24.

13. Psalm 31:24.

14. Matthew 5:5–6, paraphrased.

15. Matthew 20:20, TLB.

16. Matthew 17:22–23, paraphrased.

17. Matthew 20:20–28, paraphrased.

18. Zechariah 9:9.

19. Matthew 21:1–11, paraphrased.

20. Luke 23:55–56.

21. Luke 24:1–7, paraphrased.

22. John 20:3–17, paraphrased.

CHAPTER 9

Eunice of Lystra
Train Up a Child

I used to enjoy going down to the river just beyond Lystra. There was an ancient willow tree on the riverbank. Its shade spread like a green canopy over the soft, mossy grass. I could always count on cool breezes and warm conversation beneath its leafy awning.

Since there weren't enough Jews in our village of Lystra to support a synagogue, we would meet down by that stream to pray and to worship God. Mother Lois, my son, Timothy, and I had worn a smooth path to our favorite meeting place with God and his followers.

The name Timothy is rich with significance. It means "honoring God." Even before his birth my prayer for my son was that he should always, in every way, honor the Lord. My prayer was answered for Timothy honored, revered God! He was such a good boy. A little shy perhaps, but so polite and respectful! There never was a finer son. He was small of stature, but noble of heart. Physically he was not very strong, and he had always had trouble with his stomach. A mother's life is joy mixed with pain. The joy is her love and delight in her children; the pain, her constant concern for them.

This story takes approximately forty minutes to present orally.
For more ideas, see "Hints for Presenters" at the beginning of this book.

My mother, Lois, shared my concern. "Eunice," she would ask, "have you mixed myrrh with the wine for Timothy?" He frequently used this remedy for the upset stomach that so often plagued him.

Timothy has become quite well known, renowned, some would say. My mother and I are remembered because we brought up my son to know the Scriptures and to serve the Lord. It wasn't always easy because my husband was not a Jew. He was a Greek. He had absolutely no interest in the God whom I worshiped and loved.

"I've got gods of my own; I don't need any more," he would say. But in spite of his indifference to my devotion to the One True God, he never stood in the way of my sharing Holy Scripture with our son.

That was a real blessing because we didn't have a synagogue where I could have sent Timothy to learn the Torah, Mishna, or Midrash.[1] My favorites in all the Scriptures were the Prophets, especially Isaiah and Micah. My mother was partial to the Poetic writings, so between us, Timothy was well grounded in Scripture.

I can still hear Timothy's earnest plea, "Mother," he would say, his eyes glowing with anticipation, "tell me again about the glory of Zion!"

I would open the scroll to Isaiah and read, "A highway shall be there, and a road, and it shall be called the Highway of Holiness . . . And the ransomed of the Lord shall return, and come to Zion with singing, with everlasting joy on their heads. They shall obtain joy and gladness, and sorrow and sighing shall flee away."[2]

His eyes glowed with longing. "Mother," he would sigh, "will we ever go to Zion?"

"I don't know, son, I don't know. But someday, whether we're here in Lystra, or in Jerusalem, the Messiah will come and free us from our bondage."

Then I would turn to Isaiah Forty and read, "Behold, the Lord God shall come with a strong hand, and His arm shall rule for Him; behold His reward is with Him, and His work before Him. He will feed His flock like a shepherd; He will gather the lambs with His arm, and carry them in His bosom, and gently lead those who are with young."[3]

It was interesting that my husband, who did not object to Timothy being trained in Scripture, should have been so adamantly opposed to circumcision. "You'll not mutilate my son!" he demanded. So dear Timothy, part Jew and part Greek, was uncircumcised. I grieved, but was grateful for the blessings of Scripture and for our home and community.

Our village was on a small hill about one hundred fifty feet above a fertile valley. Iconium was to the northwest and Derbe was northeast. Both towns were considerably more significant than Lystra. Lystra was well away from the main roads of Asia Minor, so we didn't have a lot of unwanted traffic.

"You know, Eunice," my mother often reflected, "God has given us a good life in this quiet place. It's hard to believe that the Romans built this village just to regulate those mountain tribes down on Galatia's southern frontier."

"It is hard to believe, isn't it?" I said. "But I am glad that we settled here when we had to leave Israel because of the Dispersion. But, poor Timothy, how he yearns for the Zion he has never seen!"

Timothy was hardly in his teens when his father died. Frail and shy, dear Timothy became the man of our home. I worked in the fields with him while Lois took care of the household chores.

My son and I were a good team! It was one of the joys of my life to see that young man with his earnest heart and eager hands tending to all the responsibilities that had fallen on him. And never a murmur!

By the time Timothy turned fifteen, our lives had fallen into a hard-working but comfortable routine. However, things happen. Life breaks in. The routine is interrupted. When that occurs, life is never the same.

The life-changing interruption in our lives came in the form of a man, a man from Tarsus by way of Jerusalem—a man named Paul. Lois was the first member of our family to see him.

Timothy and I were in the fields. I was gathering grain while Timothy tended our small flock of sheep. I looked up from my work to see Lois running toward me. How strange, I thought. I felt a quickening in my spirit as I watched her. I ran to meet her under the sycamore tree.

"Mother!" I cried. "What is it? You startled me. Is anything wrong?"

Lois wiped the perspiration from her brow with her sleeve as she caught her breath. "They're here," she said. "Paul and Barnabas—they're in Lystra."

"Paul and Barnabas?" I cried. "The evangelists who preached in Iconium?"

"Yes," she said. "The very same!"

"Oh, Mother, how exciting!" I said, still clutching my sickle. "Miriam said that they preached that Messiah had come! And now Paul and Barnabas are here, here in Lystra? Are they really in the village?" I asked.

"They're down by the gates where the cripple always sits," she answered. "There he was," Mother continued, "as he always was, no strength in his feet, a cripple from the day he was born."

"I know, I know," I interrupted. "He has never walked. But what has that to do with Barnabas and with Paul?"

"Well, I'll tell you if you'll let me!" Mother said, her face flushed. "Paul was speaking about Messiah, quoting from the Prophets and the Psalms. And all the while the cripple watched with great interest. I saw Barnabas gesture to Paul, and as Paul went on speaking, the lame man's interest only grew more intense."

Lois drew a breath, then continued. "I felt my own interest growing. I watched as Paul turned to that unfortunate wretch and say, 'I see your faith, sir.' Then he startled all of us when, in a loud voice, he commanded, 'Stand up, straight up on your feet!'"

She grabbed my sleeve in her excitement. "Eunice! The crippled man jumped to his feet! He walked! It was a miracle."

"Oh, Mother, do you think Paul and Barnabas are prophets?" I cried.

"Well, the people down by the village gate thought they were gods!"

"Gods!" I said, incredulous.

"Yes," Lois went on. "They called Barnabas Jupiter, and addressed Paul as Mercury. The townspeople wanted to sacrifice to them. The priest from Zeus' temple, along with a great crowd of people, brought oxen and wreaths of flowers. They were going to sacrifice for Barnabas and Paul as if they were gods!

"When the prophets realized what was happening they got so upset that they tore their clothing! They said, 'We're not gods! We're men, just like you! We've come to bring you good news that you should turn from these worthless things to the living God!'"

The next day Timothy, Mother and I abandoned our usual routine. We hurried to the village in hopes of finding the evangelists so that we too could hear about Messiah.

As we made our way quickly down the path, Lois recited one of her favorite psalms, "Lift up your heads, O you gates! And be lifted up, you everlasting doors! And the King of glory shall come in. Who is this King of glory? The Lord strong and mighty, the Lord mighty in battle."[4]

I responded with another line from Scripture, "Behold! My Servant whom I uphold, My Elect One, in whom My soul delights! I have put My Spirit upon Him; He will bring forth justice to the Gentiles."[5]

And Timothy, dear Timothy added, "I am the Lord, that is My name; and My glory I will not give to another, nor My praise to graven images. Behold, the former things have come to pass and new things I declare; before they spring forth, I tell you of them."[6]

With those precious words of Scripture in our hearts, we came upon the people who had gathered around Barnabas and Paul. We stood on the fringes of the crowd, straining to hear every word.

Paul was the younger of the two men and more talkative. There was a dignified bearing about Barnabas that commanded attention, but it was Paul's words that struck responsive cords in our hearts.

"Men and women of Lystra, don't miss this—Jesus of Nazareth is the man whom God has endorsed by miracles, wonders, and signs. God did all these miracles, wonders and signs through Jesus.

"But men followed God's prearranged plan. These lawless men nailed Jesus to a cross. He was murdered! But God released him from the horrors of death and raised him back to life again, for death could not keep him in its grip.

"Do you remember what David said about him? 'I know the Lord is always with me. I will not be shaken for He is right beside me. No wonder my heart is filled with joy, and my mouth shouts his praises! My body rests in hope. For you will not leave my soul among the dead or allow your Holy One to rot in the grave.'"[7]

With eyes aglow, Paul continued, "My friends, consider this! David was not referring to himself when he spoke these words, for he both died and is buried, and his tomb is here with us to this day. But David was a prophet, and he knew God had promised with an oath that one of his own descendants would sit on his throne as the Messiah.

"David was looking into the future when he wrote these words. He was predicting the Messiah's resurrection! He was saying that the Messiah would not be left among the dead and that his body would not rot in the grave. This prophecy was speaking of Jesus whom God raised from the dead! And my friends, I am a witness. I have seen the risen Lord!"

What? Paul has seen the Lord, risen from the dead? I was astounded!

Paul paused reflectively, then stated, "Jesus, being raised up, is our Messiah—the Anointed One. He has come to seek and to save—to seek and to save *you!*"

I could feel my heart beating in the joy of this momentous occasion as Paul added solemnly, "Repent, my friends, and receive the Holy Spirit, for the promise is to you, and to your children, and to all, even those who are far away. The promise is to as many as the Lord our God will call and who will respond."

Barnabas spoke then. "Lift your eyes to heaven and pray with me to God the Father and to his Son, Jesus."

I lifted my head and raised my eyes to the azure sky dotted with the fluffy clouds of mid-morning. "O Lord," my soul sighed, "how wonderful that you have fulfilled your promise in my lifetime."

Barnabas began praying aloud, "Oh, our great and glorious Father, Almighty God, hear our prayer! We lift our heads to your heavens in praise and adoration, our hearts filled with the joy of your salvation. Thank you that your prophecies have been fulfilled in your Son, our Lord, Jesus of Nazareth, who lived and died and was raised up again by your strong and mighty hand. I pray that many here will hear your voice of salvation and answer your call to repentance. Amen."

And all assembled cried out in one voice, "Amen."

Everyone was reluctant to leave. We all pressed eagerly around the two evangelists, anxious to have a word with them about this wonderful good news.

"Did you hear what Paul said?" Timothy asked, his face aglow with anticipation.

"Oh, yes, Timothy, yes!" I responded.

Then Lois cried out in her excitement, "The Messiah! He's come! Blessed be the Lord! He allowed me to live to see the day of salvation!"

We hugged one another in our joy, casting sidelong glances toward Barnabas and Paul, hoping for the opportunity to question them further about their startling revelations. At last they were free of the townspeople, and we could have their attention.

My mother spoke first. "We are overcome with joy that you came to Lystra. All my life I have waited for the Messiah, and now you come with the glorious good news that he has indeed come. What a blessed day!"

Barnabas, who stood tall and dignified, smiled warmly at Mother Lois. "There is so much more that we would like to share with you and your fellow citizens. As the Lord allows, we will stay in Lystra and share the good news of Jesus' resurrection and redemption."

Paul added, "We see no synagogue in Lystra. Where do you meet for prayer and worship?"

It was Timothy who responded, his shyness overcome by his joy. "There is a sheltered spot down by the river," he told them. "It is our habit to meet there since there are not enough Jewish men in our town to form a synagogue."

"Very good," Paul smiled. "We'll meet with you there tomorrow at about this same time." That was the beginning of our journey with Christ.

Beginning is an interesting word, and it certainly applied to our situation, for that was the beginning. One of the teachings that Paul and Barnabas shared was the word of Jesus to a man named Nicodemus: "Unless a man is born again, he cannot enter the kingdom of heaven."

Born—begin—new beginning . . . Timothy, Lois, and I were born of the Spirit the day we met Paul and Barnabas. Our new life began, our life in Messiah.

We hoped the evangelists would stay with us forever. We learned more and more as the days and weeks went by. We established a small church and were growing in numbers and in Spirit. But word of Paul's preaching reached the ears of the Jews in Iconium and Antioch. They were not pleased with Paul's success.

It wasn't long before Lystra was visited by those rabble-rousers. The events that followed burn in my memory as a token of divine grace and human sinfulness. We had just concluded a prayer meeting and were saying shalom, when we heard the commotion in the street. We opened the door to see a crazed mob heading straight toward us. Hatred blazed from their murderous eyes. They were intent on mischief and more!

"There they are!" we heard one of the unsavory fellows shout. He was pointing a menacing finger toward Paul, contempt and malice in his eyes. We were rudely pushed aside as the mob surged forward, grabbing Paul by his arms and dragging him away in a sea of swearing ruffians.

Our small congregation followed, screaming at the intruders to stop, but to no avail. The mean-spirited thugs could not be dissuaded from their awful mission. The dust of the road rose in a fog, stinging our eyes and filling our lungs with its dry grit. Before long we were beyond the city gate, still unable to stop the invading mob.

And there, just a short distance from Lystra, the fray took on an even more sinister bent! I could not believe my eyes! How could this be happening? The scene became nightmarish and surreal, as stones gathered with hatred and malice were hurled at our dear friend and mentor! The mob was so large that they had no trouble fending off our valiant but vain attempts to aid our brother-in-Christ!

And then, as suddenly as it began, it was over. The assailants, believing their mission had been accomplished, and that Paul lay dead on the road, left the bloody scene, a swirl of insults spewing from their evil hearts and mouths.

"Oh Paul!" Timothy cried as we ran to the lifeless form of our friend and teacher. Mother Lois and I were right at his heels as he knelt in the dusty path and cradled Paul's head in his loving arms.

"He's dead!" Lois sobbed.

"Oh, precious Savior, how can this be?" I cried.

Timothy's face brightened. He looked up at me. "Mother!" he whispered hopefully. "I felt him move!" Timothy put his cheek close to Paul's mouth. "Mother, he's alive!"

The men from our group hurried to our aid, lifting Paul gently from the ground.

"Take him to our house," I said anxiously, as the men carried their precious burden.

The following days sped by in a flurry of activity as we tended Paul's wounds and prayed for his recovery. The pain he endured was skillfully masked by this courageous soldier of the Lord. As time went on, and Paul felt better, we had the benefit of his personal teaching. What a priceless treasure that was. We came to know Jesus more and more intimately through the loving teaching of our dear friend.

His words of hope still burn in my heart, "Salvation that comes from trusting Christ is already within easy reach. In fact, the Scriptures say, 'The message is close at hand; it is on your lips and in your heart.' For if you confess with your mouth that Jesus is Lord and believe in your heart that God raised him from the dead, you will be saved. For it is by believing in God, and it is by confessing with your mouth that you are saved."[8]

The time came, as we knew it must, for Paul and Barnabas to leave. Their departure was watered with our tears, but we were encouraged by the hope of their return. Soon our lives took on a new routine—one of added veneration toward the Word, constancy in prayer, and the breaking of bread.

Our community of believers was growing more united in Christ with every passing day. I noticed that Timothy expressed an even deeper devotion to the Lord than that of our dear brothers and sisters in Christ.

One day, during harvest, we were surprised by a brief visit of Paul and Barnabas. The evangelists were on their way to bring the good news of Jesus to others throughout Asia Minor. How good it was to see them once again.

"We are here, dear friends, to strengthen your souls," Barnabas told us as we gathered for prayer, fasting and worship.

"Yes," Paul agreed. "You must continue strong in the faith. There will be many trials and tribulations. But we will enter the kingdom of God."

Timothy whispered an accenting "Amen."

During our meeting, which lasted for several days, Barnabas and Paul appointed elders.

"You will need spiritual guides to help the church grow. That is what our Lord desires," he explained.

Once again we said a sad shalom to our good friends. The time had come for them to carry the message of salvation to those who had not yet heard.

Later we heard the reports of their work in Perga and Attalia. The news of their courageous witness throughout the land spread like a mountain stream after a torrential rain.

From Attalia, they sailed to Antioch where they were highly commended for the work that they had already completed. I could imagine the believers' excitement when they learned that God had opened the door of faith to the Gentiles.

"Yes, it's true," Paul announced. "God's grace is for all who would believe, Jew and Greek, male and female. Jesus died for all!"

How I longed to be in Antioch. We missed the fellowship and teaching of our brothers in the Lord, especially as their stay in Antioch was for such a long time. But the Lord kept us in Lystra where we continued to work our fields and flocks and to grow stronger in the Lord as we worshiped and prayed with other believers.

"Here's a letter from Paul and Barnabas," Lois said one day as Timothy and I came in from the fields. "They were summoned to appear before the Jerusalem Council."

"Why?" Timothy asked.

"Apparently they had to speak to the issue of circumcision. What a debate! It rocked the whole community."

Some time later Paul himself returned to Lystra. There are life-defining moments for all of us. That visit of Paul's was one of them.

It was Timothy who opened the door to Paul's knock. "Paul!" was all he could manage to say.

"How good to see you!" I added.

Mother Lois had the presence of mind to say, "Shalom, brother. Peace be with you. Come in, and bring your friend."

"Shalom!" Paul greeted with effusive warmth. "I want you to meet my friend from Jerusalem, Silas."

We embraced and greeted each other with the kiss of the Lord.

"I've heard a lot about you, Timothy," Paul said, grinning from ear to ear.

"What have you heard?" I wanted to know.

Paul addressed Timothy, still smiling. "Everywhere I went I heard how you are growing strong in the Lord. I thank our Heavenly Father for that!"

"Ah, Paul," Timothy responded. "It's all your teaching and the power of the Holy Spirit."

We sat up talking and praying long into the night. The crickets sang their plaintive song while fireflies danced in the darkness, lighting the sky for brief moments.

"O great and glorious Lord," Paul prayed, "I thank you for Timothy. I know that he sincerely trusts you, for he has the faith of his mother, Eunice, and his grandmother, Lois. You saved us and chose us to live a holy life. All glory and honor are yours. May the grace of the Lord Jesus Christ be with us. Amen."

Paul thoughtfully glanced at each of us seated around our small circle. Finally his eyes rested on Timothy's upturned face. "I have a letter from the Council regarding the matter of circumcision," he began. "It assures us that Gentiles do not have to become Jews before becoming Christians.

"In other words," Paul went on, "the only circumcision needed is the circumcision of the heart. It was Peter himself who rose up to declare, 'God, who knows the heart, acknowledged [the Gentiles], by giving them the Holy Spirit, just as He did to us, and made no distinction between us and them, purifying their hearts by faith.'"[9]

"Timothy," Paul said solemnly, "I've prayed about this matter for some time." He took Timothy's lean shoulders in his hands, his eyes looking into the very soul of my son. "I want you with me," he said. "I would like us to work together for the Lord."

I saw Timothy's eyes light up in expectation. I felt a quickening around my heart.

Paul continued, "You have such a tender heart for the Lord. And your understanding of Scriptures is unsurpassed. Your mother and grandmother have prepared you well for the mission the Lord has for you."

"Timothy," Paul cleared his throat and continued softly, "I would like you to accompany me on my next mission journey."

Those words split my heart in two! My mother-heart wanted to scream, "No, don't take my son from me!" And yet my Christian-heart submitted with joy. "My son, chosen to serve Christ and bring others to the Lord. Hallelujah!"

In the end, as Timothy turned his questioning eyes to me, I merely smiled and said, "The Holy Spirit will guide you, son. If you follow him, you are in the Lord's will and great joy will always be yours, even in the midst of trial and pain!"

"There's one more thing we need to consider," Paul said solemnly.

My son's attention was riveted on the evangelist's every word.

"Timothy, my dear brother in Christ," Paul continued, "you are a Jewish Christian. But your father was not a Jew. He was Greek. That leads to a complication. But," Paul assured, "it is not insurmountable. As a Jew, you should have been circumcised. Because you were not, some Jews consider you an irregular Jew. Gentiles see you as an irregular Gentile."

Timothy was perplexed. "Then, how can I go with you?" he asked. "Of what use can I be if I'm viewed this way by both groups?"

"There is a solution," Paul explained to my eager son, "although it is not a pleasant one. But it would cause you to no longer be between the two groups."

"What is it?" Timothy asked.

I held my breath as Paul looked into Timothy's eyes intently and uttered one word, "Circumcision."

"What?" Timothy said in a whisper. "Whose?"

"Yours," Paul answered.

My knees grew weak. I felt the blood drain from my face as I considered the ordeal Paul was asking Timothy to undergo. Before I could say anything, Timothy said, "Yes, Paul, by all means."

My shy, frail, delicate son—so courageous and strong of spirit—Timothy, "honoring God," ready to take up the mantle of greatness, ready to bring the word of God to a needy world. Timothy was ready to go anywhere—and do anything—for the sake of the kingdom.

The time for their departure came all too soon. "I'll send word, Mother," Timothy promised, and he added, "at every opportunity."

I cherished those words while Lois and I watched through tear-dimmed eyes as Paul, Silas, and our dear Timothy began their missionary journey. Of course I would miss him, but God had given me the peace that passes all understanding. And while my son worked for the Lord away from home, I worked for the Lord in Lystra.

Timothy, my loving son, was also the spiritual son of Paul, who loved Timothy more than one can imagine. Paul had special names for my son. He often referred to Timothy as "my brother" or "my fellow-worker." But the most profound and intimate was "my dear and faithful child in the Lord." Yes, Timothy was all of that. His loyalty was unsurpassed and unchallenged.

Timothy had made himself available to the Lord, and the Lord used him to further the kingdom in many ways. Timothy was key in strengthening the Corinthian church. He was used by God to establish believers in the faith in the Thessalonian church. He worked effectively with the Philippian church. He was one of God's messengers who delivered letters from Paul to churches such as the one in Colossai. And we must not forget the long years Timothy worked in the church at Ephesus.

I always had great concern for Timothy's frail health. Even Paul told him to take a little wine for his stomach. Yet, nothing stopped Timothy. His love for the Lord and his loyalty to Paul kept him striving all his life to bring the good news of salvation to all who would listen.

I grieve for the suffering, hardship, and persecution he endured. But he counted it all joy. "It is for the faith," he wrote. He was no stranger to prison or danger, but he never regretted or recanted. I'm so proud of my son who is also my brother in the Lord.

Much time has passed. I've grown old. Timothy is waiting for me. I'm ready to follow him to his new home in Heaven where Jesus went to prepare rooms for us. I am certain that Paul's and Timothy's rooms are near one another and close to Jesus, for both Paul and my Timothy arrived in heaven by way of martyrdom.

The news of Timothy's death in the year 97 was not unexpected because of his strong stand against paganism and for the cause of Christ. My Christian-heart rejoiced that he was home with the Lord. My mother-heart grieved, waiting for the time when we would be reunited.

To the end Timothy relied on the advice of his mentor, Paul, who said in his first letter to my son, "But you, O man of God . . . pursue righteousness, godliness, faith, love, patience, gentleness. Fight the good fight of faith, lay hold on eternal life, to which you were also called. . . ."[10]

Yes, Timothy, you did fight the good fight of faith. You did lay hold on eternal life. You are alive now, and soon I'll join you, and Paul, and our risen glorious Savior.

NOTES

1. In the Jewish religion, the Law is called Torah. Mishna means "repetition," and is the term for the legal opinions of respected rabbis. Midrash, meaning "commentary," are the rabbis' explanation of Scripture.

2. Isaiah 35:8a,10. Unless otherwise indicated, all Scripture quoted in this chapter is from the New King James Version of the Bible.

3. Isaiah 40:10–11.

4. Psalm 24:7–8.

5. Isaiah 42:1.

6. Isaiah 42:8–9.

7. Psalm 16:8–10, NLT.

8. Romans 10:8–10, NLT.

9. Acts 15:8–9.

10. 1 Timothy 6:11–12.

Recommended reading: Acts 14:1–16:5 and 1 and 2 Timothy

Lydia

A Baptized Believer

Look at my hands! Soft and white as wax, but with the obvious marks of age. The purple dye of my trade long washed away with the passage of time. Ahh, the purple dye—I was well known for the excellence of my much sought-after product.

"Lydia," my friends would remark, "how gifted you are, most notably in the art of making purple dye."

I brought the craft with me from Thyatira[1] when I settled in Philippi in Macedonia.[2] Sometimes I miss Thyatira and the fertile plain of the Lycus River which flows there—not that it was such a big city, but how it throbbed with commerce, especially commerce concerning purple dye. The abundance of the shellfish needed to produce the dye made the difference. Without the shellfish, there would be no purple dye.

"I thought Thyatira was noted for the madder root. It grows in abundance there, doesn't it?" Anna, a Philippian friend, asked.

"That's true," I agreed, "and it produces a fine shade of red—ah, but purple!—that's the color for royal robes. Everyone knows that it's the most desired color for the wealthy, and even for robes that adorn the gods and goddesses occupying every temple throughout the Roman Empire. It is also the color of choice for the curtains and

---

This story takes just over thirty minutes to present orally.
For more ideas, see "Hints for Presenters" at the beginning of this book.

hangings in the Hebrew temple. Everyone aspires to owning some garment or wall hanging dyed in the royal hue—purple."

Dyeing is an ancient craft. The secret formula I use has been passed down from generation to generation. Why, my dye is among the finest in all the world. Do you wonder that tanners and weavers and many others seek me out for my unique product?

Here in Philippi, I am known for my art and skill as a business-woman. Because of the demand for my rich purple dye, I am also a woman of affluence. I am keenly aware that possessing wealth is a tremendous responsibility. I have always been careful as an alms giver, and since I became a God-fearer[3] I feel privileged to share my wealth with the Hebrew people.

Since I joined their ranks as a worshiper, I have run into some problems with my trade union, "The Guild of Dyers." Especially in Thyatira, but even here, it is very strong and influential. It is, unfor-tunately, a necessary evil. Without membership in a strong guild, your social and economic success can be greatly impaired.

Since I have become a God-fearer, I have found some of their prac-tices to be in direct opposition to my new faith in the one true God, the Lord God Yahweh. All phases of our society—music, the arts, sports, even politics—were so linked to the pagan rituals demanded by the guilds, that most of my business associates made serious accommodations to those pagan practices.[4] After all, they wanted to be "respectable" members of society. So did I. When I learned, how-ever, that the pagan rites were an abomination to the Lord God, I abandoned the practices, at great personal risk I might add.

I substituted the pagan customs with prayer—individual and cor-porate. Other God-fearers, Jewish believers, and I would meet for that very purpose down by the river. I loved it there, so quiet and away from the crowded hill section of Philippi. Philippi is larger than Thyatira. The city boasts an enormous forum, two prodigious tem-ples and numerous public buildings. Why, we even have a magnifi-cent open-air theater and an ornate arch about a mile west of the city.

"That's odd," I thought when I first saw the impressive structure. Why would the Romans build such a classic arch so far from the city? Not being one to deny my curiosity, I asked Anna.

Her answer puzzled me. "Rumor has it," she said, "that it's a zon-ing marker meant to restrict undesirable religious groups from meet-ing within the city."

"Do they mean the Jews?" I asked.

"I don't know," was her response. "But if it were meant for us Jews, it would include you, too, because even though you're a Gentile, you are a God-fearer."

"Is that restriction the reason we meet for prayer down by the river?"

"Perhaps," she said. "But besides that, there aren't enough Jews and God-fearers in Philippi to support a synagogue."[5]

We fell into silence as we continued on our way toward our revered meeting place. As we neared the river, the ebb and flow of our friends' voices cascaded above the ripples of the river caressing the bank. Anna and I instinctively hastened our steps in our desire to be with our friends and begin the prayer meeting.

We made our way through the stand of trees, anxious to break free of its shade and enter the brightness of the beach. Our hurried steps brought us to the water's edge at last.

"Shalom, Anna," the women greeted. "How do you fare, Lydia?" they added.

As I looked into the radiant faces of my companions, I was struck by a sudden realization. Why, I mused, they are as different from one another as tears and smiles, shadow and sunshine. But they are, each and every one, filled with an ardent love for Yahweh, and a gratitude for our God's promises.

"Come, Lydia," Abi said, interrupting my reverie. "How does it fare with you? We missed you at our last meeting. Are you well? Is your business prospering?"

"So many questions, Abi," I laughed. "But I am grateful for your concern. Yes, all is well with my health and my business. It was my business that kept me from our last meeting, a fact that I truly lament. I was eager to conclude a certain transaction, one for which I had prepared for some time. When the opportunity presented itself, I took advantage of the timing.

"Ah, but my friends," I added solemnly, "that was the last business transaction I'll make that interferes with our prayer meeting."

"That's good," Anna said. "Besides," she added, "your purple dye is the finest in all the land, so I would think your clients would be willing for you to serve them at your convenience."

"Thank you for those kind words," I said. "I know that there are some matters that must take precedence over others, and Yahweh has become my top priority."

We stood on the bank, bathed in sunshine and caressed by the river breeze. We called upon the Lord. The prayer meeting began in earnest.

It was Abi who began, "God be merciful to us and bless us, and cause His face to shine upon us, that your way may be known on earth, your salvation among all nations."[6]

An unfamiliar, masculine voice continued the psalm, "Let the peoples praise you, O God; let all the peoples praise you. Oh, let the nations be glad and sing for joy! For you shall judge the people righteously, and govern the nations on earth."[7]

I beheld the strangers who had joined our circle. Their eyes were fixed upon the heavens. The man continued praying the noble psalm, "Let the peoples praise you, O God; let all the peoples praise you. Then the earth shall yield her increase; God, our own God, shall bless us. God shall bless us, and all the ends of the earth shall fear Him."[8]

We stood in wonder at this stranger and his companions. The might of his voice belied the smallness of his stature. The strength of his gaze demanded our attention.

"I am Paul," he said, "and these are my dear friends and fellow travelers, Timothy, Silas, and Doctor Luke." He motioned us to be seated. He sat on the grassy slope as well.

"Shalom," we greeted as we took our places around them.

"Welcome," I added. "I am Lydia." I took the liberty then to introduce the other worshipers to Paul and his friends.

"Ah," Paul said, "It is clear why the Lord has sent me to be among you."

"Why, indeed?" Anna asked.

"While in Troas," he explained, "a vision came to me at night. A man appeared to me and entreated me to come to Macedonia, 'to help us,' he said. I made haste to come to you.

"We sailed from Troas on a straight course to Samothrace. The next day we went on to Neapolis, and from there, we came straight here.[9]

"Scripture says, 'Therefore the Lord will wait, that he may be gracious to you; and therefore he will be exalted, that he may have mercy on you. For the Lord is a God of justice; blessed are all those who wait for him.'[10]

"My friends, your wait is over. Scripture further tells us, 'Behold, the Lord God shall come with a strong hand, and His arm shall rule for Him. Behold, His reward is with Him, and His work before

Him. He will feed His flock like a shepherd; He will gather the lambs with His arm, and carry them in His bosom, and gently lead those who are with young.'[11]

"I have good news, my friends. The Lord God has come! Isaiah told us about him in his prophecies, 'Surely He has borne our griefs and carried our sorrows; yet we esteemed Him stricken, smitten by God, and afflicted. *(I remembered the passage!)* But He was wounded for our transgressions, He was bruised for our iniquities; the chastisement for our peace was upon Him, and by His stripes we are healed. All we like sheep have gone astray; we have turned every one to his own way; and the Lord has laid on Him the iniquity of us all.'"[12]

I felt a thrill of anticipation as Paul continued, "Jesus of Nazareth, the Messiah, has come!" In his excitement, Paul rose to his feet. "The grave could not hold the Savior! He is risen, the first fruits of those that sleep!"[13]

"Who is this Jesus of Nazareth?" I wondered.

"He has fulfilled the Scriptures! He was born of a virgin; he was without sin. And yet, my friends, he took my sins, your sins upon himself when he went to the cross!"

The cross! my mind screamed. That dreadful instrument of doom? How could I, or anyone, be saved by one dying on that cruel device of death?

"Yes!" Paul continued, seeming to have read my thoughts. "Jesus went to the cross! He died for our sins according to the Scriptures, he was buried, and he rose again on the third day according to the Scriptures. Jesus, who had died, was seen—alive—by Peter and the other disciples. After that, he was seen by more than five hundred followers of the way, all at the same time. Then he was seen by James, then by all the apostles."

Paul took a breath and added, almost as a prayer, "Then, last of all, he was seen by me, the least of all the apostles. I am not worthy to be called his apostle because I persecuted the church. But by the grace of God, I am what I am, and his grace toward me was not in vain; for I labor more abundantly than the rest. But it is not I, but the grace of God which is with me. We preach that you might believe! Jesus Messiah has risen from the dead! Believe and be saved!"[14]

"Paul!" I said, rising to my feet. "I do believe! The long-awaited Messiah has come!"

"Then," Paul said, taking my hand in his, "You must be baptized."

"Yes, Paul," I agreed. "I will go at once to fetch all those in my household, kin and servant alike. They, too, must receive the blessing offered by the Lord."

He released my hand. I turned and retraced my steps as quickly as I could, praying all the way. I quickly gathered everyone in my household, anxious to tell them what had happened. I'm not sure they understood my words, but there was no missing my joy.

"Come," I said at last, "we must go down to the river. Paul is waiting for us." Without another word, I turned and made my way down the well-worn path to the river's edge, my kindred and servants following close behind.

Abi, Anna, all my friends, were waiting for us, along with Paul and his companions.

"Lydia," he called, "the hour has come. Are you ready?"

"Yes," I said, breathless, not only from my hurried return, but from the excitement and exhilaration of the occasion as well.

"Come," he said, leading me gently into the cool water. We made our way slowly until we were waist deep in the quiet river. He cradled my head in his left arm, holding my hands with his right. I relaxed against his grip as he lowered me into the water, saying, "I baptize you in the name of the Father, the Son, and the Holy Spirit."

A surge of God's cleansing power overwhelmed me as I died to sin and was raised with Jesus in that instant of purification.

"Praise God!" were my first words as I was helped up out of the water.[15]

Hadassah, my handmaiden, wrapped a tunic about my shoulders. She was next to be baptized, followed by Mary, my cook, and one by one, all the others. The shivering had stopped by the time Abi went into the river with Paul.

Finally, we all stood there, singing a psalm of praise for God's forgiving grace. "O God, my heart is steadfast; I will sing and give praise, even with my glory . . . I will praise You, O Lord, among the peoples, and I will sing praises to You among the nations. For Your mercy is great above the heavens, and Your truth reaches to the clouds. Be exalted, O God, above the heavens, and Your glory above all the earth."[16]

"You see, do you not, Paul," I said, "that I am faithful to the Lord?"

"Yes," he agreed, a smile creasing the corners of his eyes.

"Then, Paul," I urged, "come, you and your companions, stay with me at my home."

"But, Lydia," he argued, "there's Doctor Luke, and Timothy and Silas. Can you accommodate all of us?"

"My home is spacious," I replied. "There is more than enough room. You would honor me and my household by staying with us. Please, Paul, come."

I could tell that I had won the argument by the sweeping smile that lit up his face. "Yes Lydia," he said. "But it is I who am honored to be your guest. Thank you."

Paul's stay at my home was a time of spiritual growth and rejoicing. No one knew the Torah, the history, and the Prophets as did Paul. I had known nothing until I became a God-fearer, and I learned how little I really knew before I met Paul. It was exhilarating to hear Paul unfold God's work among the chosen people, and even more exciting to learn that God's grace was meant for all who would believe.

"Tell me more about Jesus," I said one day as we started on our way to the riverbank. I could never hear enough about the Savior, nor could his companions who walked with us. And it was clear that Paul never tired of speaking about him.

"Our Savior was the consummate story-teller," Paul began. "His parable of the lost sheep is among my favorites. Jesus spoke of a man who had a hundred sheep. But when one of them gets lost, he leaves the ninety-nine to find the lost one. He finds it, and carries it back on his shoulder, rejoicing! He calls all his friends and neighbors to rejoice with him, saying, 'Rejoice with me, for I have found my sheep which was lost!'"

"That's beautiful," I said, "but, tell me, Paul, what was the point of his story?"

"Well," Paul said, "Jesus went on to explain that just like the shepherd who found the lost sheep, there will be more joy in heaven over one sinner who repents than over the ninety-nine others who are righteous and didn't stray away!"[17]

"How wonderful, Paul!" I said. "I was like the lost sheep. And now, there is joy in heaven because I have repented and belong to Jesus!"

He began to relate another parable of Jesus, but was interrupted by a slave girl who began following us, shouting, "These men are servants of the Most High God and proclaim to us the way of salvation."

"I'm sorry for the distraction, Paul," I said. "She has a spirit of divination. I'm afraid her masters use her for their own profit."

We had almost arrived at our destination before the girl left us, still shouting about Paul and his companions. It took a while to quiet our own spirits after that, but at last we had the marvelous calm of Jesus and our time of prayer began.

After that, every time we made our way through the city and the outer gate, the possessed girl followed, shouting. Her words never changed. They were always the same: "These men are servants of the Most High God and proclaim to us the way of salvation."

The daily pronouncements were annoying and frustrating. As Paul, Silas, and I walked along, we tried to ignore it. But Paul wanted to put a stop to it.

"Enough!" he said, stopping so suddenly that the girl almost collided with him. He turned to face his tormentor. She stood resolutely, unmoved, unafraid, looking squarely into Paul's fixed gaze. I watched, transfixed, as he slowly raised an arm to heaven.

His voice boomed with the authority of God Almighty, "Spirit," he said, "I command you, in the name of Jesus Christ, come out of her!"

Her defiant look was instantly replaced with a mask of confusion and anxiety. She turned and ran, sobbing.

Without another word, we made our way to the riverbank and prayer. After some time, however, we heard voices in the thicket. We all turned to see who it might be. A group of men emerged from the stand of trees.

The thugs grabbed Paul and Silas roughly, shouting, "You wretched men! You have stolen our livelihood."

"What do you mean?" Silas managed.

"Our slave girl, that's what! She can no longer divine the future, thanks to you. We are ruined. But, you will be, too, you can count on that!"

We tried to stop them, but they pushed us rudely away and dragged Paul and Silas off toward Philippi. We ran behind, begging for their release, but to no avail.

"Oh, Lydia," Anna said, "they're taking them to the magistrate. See, he's there in the marketplace."

We stayed as close as we could, but it became difficult because of the increasing number of people crowding the agora. I strained to hear the charges that were being brought against our friends.

"What did he say, Anna?" I asked.

"Listen, Lydia," she said, putting a finger to her lips.

I did as Anna said. I could hear the raspy voice of one of the abductors. "These men," he shouted, "these Jews come here and cause an uproar in the whole city. They have been teaching people to do things which are against our Roman laws!"

With that, my friends and I were pushed roughly aside as the mob surged forward. I watched in horror as Paul and Silas were stripped to the waist. More horror followed. Our mentors were beaten severely. I cried in anguish, but was helpless to go to their aid. Then, beaten and bloody, our Christian brothers were led away to prison.[18] The crowd dispersed.

"Come," I said, "let's go to my home. We need to pray."

We left the marketplace and made our way to my home, a sanctuary for those who had come to know the Lord. Not a word was spoken as we tread the weary way. I heard Abi sobbing quietly. Anna put a comforting arm about her shoulders to console her lifelong friend. At last we arrived at our destination. Joseph, my porter, held the door open wide for us to enter. As soon as the last guest was inside, he closed and locked the door. I led my friends to the spacious courtyard.

"Please, dear friends," I said, "take seats. We must pray for our brothers."

"Yes," Abi said, tears glistening in her dark eyes, "they have been wrongfully imprisoned." She began weeping again.

I offered refreshments, but everyone refused, so we began to pray. It was Anna who lifted the first prayerful petition. "Arise, O Lord! O God, lift up Your hand! Do not forget the humble. Why do the wicked renounce God? He has said in his heart, 'You will not require an account.' But You have seen it, for You observe trouble and grief, to repay it by Your hand. The helpless commits himself to You; you are the helper of the fatherless."[19]

One after another, we prayed for the deliverance of our friends. Before long we abandoned our couches and fell to our knees. Two or three women lay prostrate on the stone floor.

Around midnight I felt the first tremor. Earthquake! We prayed more ardently than ever. "God," I prayed wordlessly, "are you telling us something in the might of your works?" The tremors grew more violent, and we became frightened. And then, in a matter of moments, it was over. I looked at my friends. They had regained their composure, as had I.

We resumed our prayers. "Then the earth shook and trembled; the foundations of the hills also quaked and were shaken . . . [but] You have also given me the shield of Your salvation; Your right hand has held me up . . ."[20]

That was the first time we held an all-night prayer vigil, but you can be sure, it was not the last. We were to learn the power of prayer with the dawning of a new day, for just as the gloom of night faded in the eastern sky, my porter led Paul and Silas into the courtyard! What rejoicing. What tears of relief.

"Shalom, Paul! Shalom, Silas!" we chorused. We resumed our circle, but this time, it was around Paul and Silas. "Are you all right?" I asked. "What did they do to you? How did you gain your freedom?"

Paul laughed, "One question at a time."

We all laughed, the sweet laughter of relief. Then Silas began to relate the events. "We were thrown into prison," he said. "The police told the jailer not to let us escape. 'Make sure!' he said. So we were taken to the inner dungeon and our feet were clamped into stocks."

"Yes," Paul added. "But it wasn't so bad, was it Silas?"

"No," was the response, "it gave us the opportunity to pray."

"And sing psalms," Paul said. "You can be sure the other prisoners were listening. I even thought I heard one join in."

"Then," Silas said excitedly, "right around midnight, the Lord provided a great show for us."

Paul was laughing again. "An earthquake! It was a big one—so big that the prison was shaken to its foundations. All the doors flew open, and the chains fell off. Not only ours, but every prisoner's. The force of the earthquake opened all the prison doors. We could have walked right out. The jailer came rushing in."

"He was terrified," Silas said. "He was sure that all the prisoners, including we, had escaped. So he drew out his sword and was about to kill himself."

"But," Paul added, "I shouted to him, 'Don't do that. No one has left. We're all here!' He got a lantern and came into the dungeon. He was visibly shaken. He was trembling.

"He fell to his knees before us. 'Come on,' he said, 'let's get out of here.' We made our way up the stone steps, now badly damaged from the earthquake. When we exited the dungeon, he said, 'Sirs, what must I do to be saved?' We told him that he must believe in the Lord Jesus Christ, and he would be saved. We shared the good news of salvation with him, and with everyone in his household."

"It was glorious," Silas added. "He washed our wounds. And then he and his household were all baptized. We went into his house where they prepared a meal for us."

"What rejoicing," Paul said. "Every single person in the jailer's house came to repentance, assured that Jesus is the Savior.

"In the morning he told us that the police ordered him to let us go. 'You're free. Go in peace.' he said. But I told him that we had been beaten publicly, without a trial, and we had been jailed. 'We're Roman citizens[21] and, now, they want us to leave secretly? Certainly not! Let them come themselves to release us!'

"That shook up the officials!" Paul laughed.

"It surely did," Silas said. "They came to the jail themselves. You should have seen them! They led us out of prison personally and gave us a public apology."

"They begged us to leave Philippi," Paul added with a hearty laugh.

"Oh, Paul," I said, "you're not going to leave, are you?"

"I'm afraid so," he said. "We must go to Thessalonica. Besides, Lydia, there is a strong church established here in Philippi. It's thriving and growing. And I know that even the jailer and his family will worship with you."

Paul, Timothy and Silas left that very afternoon. I thank our Lord that Doctor Luke remained with us. Still, it was difficult to see the others go.

"We must," Paul said. "The good news of redemption needs to be brought to others. And God has appointed me to the mission of bringing that Word to the Gentiles."

It would be five years before we would see our dear brother in Christ again. I think about those years often. Philippi is not a Christian-friendly city, but by the grace of God, we persevered.

"Lydia," Anna said one Sabbath as we waited for the others, "how gracious of you to open your home for worship. It's perfect for meeting with our brothers and sisters in the Lord."

"Oh Anna," I replied, "it surely is a blessing for me. The Lord has so abundantly provided for me. This home is his. My greatest joy is to worship and serve him."

It wasn't long before the others began arriving. It was exciting to see how God was working in Philippi. More people joined our fellowship with every passing day. But this meeting was to be even more special than all the previous ones. We were about to have a special visit that Sabbath day.

An unaccountable hush fell over the worshipers. I turned to see why. Our dear friend had joined us!

"Paul!" I exclaimed, rushing to his open arms. "Peace be with you."

"And with your household," he said, a twinkle in his eyes. "I see your household has grown since I've seen you last." His hearty laugh filled the house.

Before long Paul was surrounded by the entire congregation. Everyone wanted to be near him—to touch him.

"I have come," Paul announced, "to celebrate the Passover with you." With that, a cheer rose from all assembled.

I often recall the days that followed. Of course, re-reading Paul's letter is a source of joy for all of us here in Philippi. Can you imagine? Paul was in prison when he penned that beautiful epistle, and he wrote about joy! It is clear that Paul's rejoicing is in the fact that he has gained Christ. He says he considers anything he has lost for the sake of Jesus to be rubbish.

Paul wrote with thanks for the gifts we sent, calling them, a "sweet-smelling aroma, an acceptable sacrifice, well pleasing to God."[22]

And now, I look forward to the day when " . . . at the name of Jesus every knee should bow . . . and that every tongue should confess that Jesus Christ is Lord, to the glory of God the Father."[23]

With joy I bow my knee to Jesus. With humility I confess that he is Lord. With gratitude I give all the glory to God the Father. And that, my friends, is my prayer for you. God bless you. Amen.

NOTES

1. Thyatira was located in the region that is modern Turkey.

2. Macedonia is modern-day Greece.

3. A God-fearer was a Gentile who worshiped the Hebrew God.

4. Pagan practices included feasts honoring pagan gods, eating meat sacrificed to pagan gods, and immoral sexual acts.

5. A minimum of ten Jewish men were needed to establish a synagogue, so where such a "quorum" was absent, people gathered in other, more informal meeting places to study Scripture and worship God together.

6. Psalm 67:1,2. All Scripture quoted in this chapter is from the New King James Version, unless otherwise noted.

7. Psalm 67:3–4.

8. Psalm 67:5–7.

9. Acts 16:9–13, paraphrased.

10. Isaiah 30:18.

11. Isaiah 40:10–11.

12. Isaiah 53:4.

13. 1 Corinthians 15:20.

14. 1 Corinthians 15:3–11, paraphrased.

15. Lydia was the first known convert to Christianity in Europe.

16. Psalm 108:1–5.

17. Luke 15:4–7, paraphrased.

18. Acts 16:16–23, paraphrased.

19. Psalm 10:12–14.

20. Psalm 18:7,35.

21. Free-born citizens of the Roman Empire were entitled to a trial and should not have been thrown into prison without a hearing.

22. Philippians 4:18.

23. Philippians 2:10–11.